The Essential Gui

Beachcombing
and the Strandline

By the same authors
IN THE COMPANY OF SEAHORSES

Published in 2015 by
Wild Nature Press Ltd

Registered address
7 Sandy Court,
Ashleigh Way,
Plymouth
PL7 5JX

Reprinted with corrections in 2016

A CIP catalogue record for this book is available from the British Library.

ISBN 978-0-9573946-7-4

Designed by Julie Dando
Printed and bound in Slovenia on behalf of Latitude Press

10 9 8 7 6 5 4

www.wildnaturepress.com

The Essential Guide to
Beachcombing
and the Strandline

Steve Trewhella and Julie Hatcher

WILD
NATURE
PRESS

Contents

This book is dedicated to our children and grandchildren who have accompanied us to the beach on numerous occasions, helping us to scour the strandline for treasures, patiently posing for photographs and frequently opening our fridge door to find seashore stuff in place of tasty treats; and in memory of Sonny the dog, who hated pebble beaches with a passion but was always delighted when the car door opened to reveal a wide expanse of sand.

Acknowledgements

We have spent many years visiting beaches all around the country in search of both the common and the more unusual flotsam and jetsom stranded on the shoreline. There is a lot we have yet to find. Beachcombing has been and will continue to be a lifelong passion and has introduced us to some of the most interesting characters imaginable, who have both inspired and encouraged us to delve ever deeper into the subject.

We were lucky enough to know Nick and Jane Darke who fuelled an already developing interest in beachcombing by introducing us to long-haul drift, which they had been collecting and researching from their Cornish home for many years. Together they produced the award-winning documentary film *The Wrecking Season* about their beachcombing finds and experiences, which acts as an inspiration to any would-be beachcomber, as it did to us. Sadly, Nick passed away shortly after making the film. Jane's passion for the coast continues.

Dr Paul Gainey has helped us enormously over the years with his exhaustive knowledge of natural history, and he has become a good friend. He has allowed us to photograph some of his considerable collection of natural beach finds and has contributed his own photographs for our book. Whether it be identifying a 2mm long beetle, an unusual strandline plant or a drift seed, his all-encompassing expertise has been invaluable.

John Hunnisett's expertise on insects has helped us on many occasions to identify those we have found in the strandline. The labour-intensive microscope work involved in naming a species from the number of hairs on its leg or the length of its antennae requires dedication beyond the call of duty. Without his help we would not have been able to include half the invertebrates in the strandline habitat section.

For her assistance in finding and identifying a range of marine species, we are indebted to Dr Lin Baldock. As well as accompanying us on the beach in all weathers, searching inside driftwood logs and even dragging sections of them off the beach for further investigation, she has also contributed her own photographs for our book.

The identification of non-native exotic molluscs for inclusion in the book was carried out by Dr Graham Oliver and Anna Holmes of the National Museum of Wales and we are indebted to both. Julie Dando and Marc Dando at Wild Nature Press for believing in us and helping make our vision of this book a reality.

A variety of people are now running beachcombing sites on social media and these have been useful in alerting us to the presence of stranded items around the country that we might otherwise have missed. We are grateful to all the people who have posted photographs of their beach finds on this network.

A number of people have helped by supplying photographs or alerting us to recent strandings and we thank them for their support – David Fenwick, Sue Scott, Rob Holmes, Richard Fabbri and Fergus Granville.

We would also like to thank our friends Dr Ken Collins and Jenny Mallinson for their support, along with Dr Curtis Ebbesmeyer.

Introduction

The beach strandline is the point where land meets sea, and visually marks the highest point of the tide. It is a place to discover rare marine treasures washed ashore by the waves, and to find items of infinite interest and fascination, but is also a home, and a source of food and shelter to some of the UK's rarest and most threatened wildlife.

With this book, we hope to share our passion for exploring the strandline and inspire others, whether they be active families, dog walkers, bird watchers or beach strollers, to get out and enjoy the pleasure of beachcombing. Who can forget the delight of discovering their first mermaid's purse on the beach and imagining the unearthly, watery world beneath the waves from which it came?

Beachcombing is an activity to delight all ages, from toddlers picking up pretty seashells to hardened naturalists uncovering exotic creatures carried here from foreign shores, or artists collecting sea-worn driftwood and romantics decorating their garden with colourful fishing buoys.

What is the strandline?

The beach strandline is made up of marine debris, mainly detached seaweed, that has floated ashore on the waves and been deposited on the beach as the tide retreats. As well as seaweed it can contain all manner of organic debris, including seashells, eggcases and bones of marine animals, driftwood and plant remains washed into the sea from cliffs and rivers, and increasingly, man-made items from plastic litter to discarded fishing gear and shipping waste.

Where does the material come from?

The bulk of material forming the strandline is fairly local in origin and the source will depend on the currents and adjacent seabed geology. Beaches close to estuaries and river mouths may contain a lot of terrestrial plant material carried there from inland, while those facing the ocean may receive a fair percentage of long-haul debris, sometimes from as far afield as North America.

Sandy beaches with predominantly sandy seabeds offshore may accumulate a limited amount of seaweed and have strandlines composed mainly of seashells or hydroids, whereas those along rocky coastlines can often be piled high in mounds of kelp.

Busy tourist beaches may contain a lot of picnic litter, while those adjacent to busy shipping lanes or intensive fishing activity may tend to collect fishing gear and shipping debris.

What can we learn from what is found?

By inspecting what washes up on a beach strandline, we can tell a lot about the local marine environment. For example, by examining the types of mermaid's purses collected we might be able to identify a ray spawning area nearby, or if the strandline is made up mostly of seagrass (a marine flowering plant) rather than seaweed it would indicate a shallow, sandy seabed colonised by seagrass meadows just offshore. The types of seashells decorating the strandline will also give clues as to the type of seabed as well as what lives there.

Some drift items may have travelled from across the ocean and are termed 'long-haul drift'. These might include seaweeds, drift seeds, exotic animals and man-made items such as fishing gear and litter. It is sometimes possible to trace these objects to their point of origin, for example fishing equipment may be marked with the name or registration number of the fisherman who owned it, or it may be of a type that is only used in a particular area. It might even have a date stamped on it. Exotic sea beans may be endemic to a distant country that can be identified as the source. From these objects we can learn something about how ocean currents work and the time it takes for drift items to cross the ocean.

Occasionally two or more long-haul drift items may wash ashore on a UK beach within metres of one another, having crossed thousands of miles of ocean. Incredible as this seems, it shows that 'parcels' of water travel over long distances as one body, keeping the items contained in them together despite the fluid nature of the sea.

WATER PARCELS

Water is fluid and we assume that the movement of wind, waves, tides and ocean currents mixes and stirs it up so that it is homogenous – like when you pour orange squash into a glass of water and stir it. In reality, within the vast body of the ocean there are discrete parcels of water that can be distinguished from the sea surrounding them by a slight difference in temperature (up to 1°C) and therefore also by a difference in salinity and density.

These parcels of water can travel across the ocean and, even after colliding with other water parcels, remain intact. Oceanographer Curtis Ebbesmeyer explains the phenomenon as 'They travel through the water as clouds float through air.'

When is the best time for beachcombing?

Beachcombing is an activity that can be enjoyed at any time, and you never know what you might find. The strandline varies from season to season depending on what is happening in the sea at particular times of year. Empty, or sometimes live, eggcases of sea creatures can be washed up en masse following spawning, and seasonal seaweeds might dominate strandlines for short periods as they approach the end of their growing season.

If you are hoping to find unusual or exotic animals, then the best beachcombing is to be had following a period of stormy weather. Large waves can catch seabed creatures out and throw them up onto the beach from the shallows where they live. Starfish and Sea Mice are good examples. Prolonged onshore winds driving in from the Atlantic are most likely to bring oceanic visitors such as By-the-wind Sailors, goose barnacles or even sea beans from Florida or the Caribbean.

Why are there multiple strandlines?

There is usually more than one strandline on the beach at any given time. This is because the tides vary throughout the month, some reaching higher up the shore than others, and consequently depositing their material at a higher level than subsequent tides.

Tides are governed by the moon and sun and their relative position to the Earth. At times of new and full moon, when the Earth, sun and moon are all in alignment and their gravitational pull on the oceans are combined, the tidal range is larger, which means the low tide is lower and the high tide is higher on the shore. These are called Spring Tides. At times of half-moon, the moon and sun form right angles with the Earth so that the gravity of the moon and sun are pulling in opposing directions. The result is that the tidal range is smaller – low tide is not so low and the high tide not so high on the shore. These are Neap Tides.

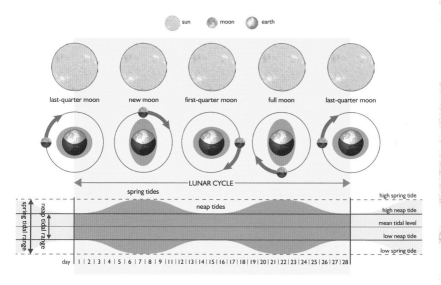

The result of this variation in tidal height is to leave multiple strandlines, but which is the best one to investigate? The freshest strandline is likely to be of most interest and should contain a wider variety of objects. Older strandlines may have been picked clean by seabirds and other beachcombers, or may have been partially covered in wind-blown sand. Some lighter items may have been dispersed by strong winds and blown to the back of the beach. However this doesn't mean they are not of interest – some interesting objects may still be found on them.

An extraordinary wildlife habitat

The strandline is predominantly made up of organic debris and as such provides food and shelter to an unusual wildlife community. Bacteria coating the surface of the seaweed starts the process of decomposition, just as happens to leaf litter on a woodland floor. This provides an abundant source of food for small invertebrates such as Sand Hoppers and seaweed flies, and mites which are almost too small for the naked eye to see. These are preyed upon by beetles, centipedes and spiders, and so on up the food chain to birds, small rodents and bats.

Rock Pipit feeding on seaweed fly maggot

At high tide, marine invertebrates continue the recycling process, adding vital nutrients to the intertidal and shallow water marine ecosystem and providing abundant food for fish such as mullet and bass.

The decomposed organic material becomes incorporated into beach sediments and enables hardy pioneer beach plants such as oraches, Sea Rocket and Sea Sandwort to colonise. These in turn collect more beach material such as wind-blown sand and organic debris. Eventually a succession of plants may colonise and on some beaches sand dune formation begins. This colonisation attracts a whole new community of wildlife and helps stabilise the mobile beach material, ultimately providing a natural coastal defence.

Beach strandlines have not been widely studied and as such are home to rarely recorded species which are often found nowhere else. At the boundary between land and sea the strandline can be a harsh environment. Washed by waves and blown by strong winds, it is an arid, salty habitat with limited fresh water, where only the most specialised plants and animals can survive.

Threats

Some strandlines have been exploited by man for centuries for their seaweed, which is used as fertiliser on farmland. Nowadays, amenity beaches are often mechanically cleaned to remove not only the man-made rubbish but also the decomposing seaweed which tourists find distasteful. Unfortunately, this process removes the whole wildlife community, leaving these beaches all but devoid of life, and threatening populations of many endemic species.

In other areas, coastal development and sea defences built behind the beach are causing 'coastal squeeze' as beach environments are prevented from retreating landward in the face of rising sea-levels. Wildlife has nowhere to go, trapped in a narrow strip between the sea and hard defences, and may be squeezed out of existence.

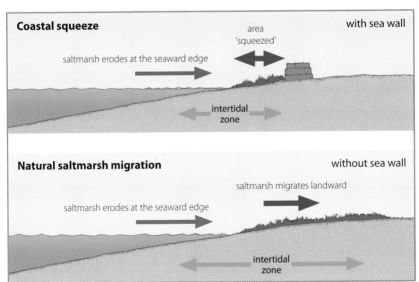

Kit list

As your interest in beachcombing develops, you might find it useful to carry some of the following items with you.

It is also worth remembering that beaches tend to be very exposed to the weather and offer little opportunities for shelter, either from wind and rain, or from strong sunlight. It is important to wear appropriate clothing, hat and footwear and take waterproofs and/or suncream. A drink is essential as you may find you walk a lot further than you expected. For this reason a tide table book or app on your phone is also a necessary item to avoid being cut off by the rising tide.

While you are on the beach, it is good practice to do your bit by collecting any litter you find in a carrier bag, for safe disposal or recycling. This is a good habit to get into and sets a good example for others.

Consider carrying the following:

Bags – one for collecting your finds and one for removing litter from the beach

Magnifier or hand lens

Camera or phone camera

Notepad and pen

Penknife

Binoculars

Specimen pots – for small fragile objects

Magnifying pot – for identifying and observing strandline invertebrates

Pooter – for collecting strandline invertebrates

Head torch – for evening safaris

Tweezers – for removing shells or other items from logs and litter

Drink – preferably in a re-usable bottle

Tide table book

Antibacterial hand gel – if you will be eating lunch after picking amongst the strandline

Collecting and recording your finds

Depending on your interests, you might decide to start a collection of some of your beachcombing finds. Fishing buoys come in a variety of styles and colours and are often used for decorating coastal-themed gardens. Items such as seashells and crab moults make attractive interior decorations and provide long-lasting memories of your trips to the coast. Collections can also be used for reference to familiarise yourself with the species and objects on the beaches you visit.

Beachcombing finds, both natural and man-made, are inspirational for creating artwork. Handmade art can give the home a unique and quirky atmosphere and is fun to do. Not only does this provide a more personal alternative to shop-bought items but also plays a role in removing, recycling and re-using man-made waste from the environment.

Large-scale removal of natural items is not recommended as these often

play an essential role in the strandline ecosystem. In particular, shells and driftwood offer shelter to many animals and should be collected sparingly. Many are also essential components of the beach itself, breaking down to form sand. Man-made debris such as rope, netting and plastic, although offering temporary shelter, is best removed, as the long-term threats it produces far out-weigh any short-term benefits.

Strandline recording

The naturalist in you may like to keep a record of your beachcombing finds, as a reference tool. By creating a beachcomber's logbook you can record your memories as well as notable species and events, tying them in with photographs taken at the time. Over time you may notice patterns emerging – certain times of year that are more productive and which beaches are best for particular species or objects.

A network of beachcombers around the UK, and indeed the world, link up through social media and share their knowledge and records. Photographs can be uploaded for help with identification. Interesting strandings and events are also shared, alerting other beachcombers to keep a watchful eye in their area.

Keeping safe

Beaches can be hazardous places for a number of reasons, and it is important to keep this in mind before heading out on a beachcombing trip. Exposure to the weather, the sea and tides, and unstable cliffs all present dangers to the unwary visitor. In order to keep safe we advise taking the following precautions.

Check tide times for the beach you are visiting before venturing out. At high tide the beach, or parts of it, may be inaccessible, or you may be cut off by a rising tide. Tide times for the week ahead are available online, or you should be able to purchase a tide book for the year at a local fishing tackle shop or chandlers.

Check the weather forecast for your area and dress and pack accordingly. A cold, wet beachcomber is an unhappy beachcomber. In storm conditions, be aware that freak waves may reach much higher up the beach than anticipated.

Beware of cliff falls and mud slides – in some parts of the country cliff falls and mud slides can be frequent and occur with no warning. It is always advisable to keep a safe distance from the foot of cliffs to avoid being hit by falling rocks or getting stuck in soft mud.

Beware of soft mud or sinking sand underfoot especially in estuaries the beach material may be very soft when the tide is out and should be avoided.

Carry a mobile phone in case of emergency situations but be aware that signal coverage can be patchy around the coast.

Wash hands or use anti-bacterial hand gel after handling dead animals or other strandline debris, especially before eating.

Beaches

Every beach is unique. We all have a favourite beach, or perhaps different favourites for different reasons. Some are best suited for a particular activity, or tend to collect the rarest drift animals. Some beaches are popular because they face west, offering plenty of sunshine and wonderful sunsets, and others are special because they provide space and solitude.

Generally beaches can be categorised by the material from which they are made – sandy, rocky, shingle or maerl.

Sandy beaches

Sandy beaches at first glance may appear to be much of a muchness but in fact each beach has its own unique blend of material. Sand is composed of two different elements – biogenic particles from ground-down seashells, skeletons and micro-organisms; and minerals from eroded rocks. Of the latter the most common type is in the form of quartz, although many other types of mineral can be mixed in depending on the local geology. Some beaches, on close inspection, can be found to be made up mostly of calcified remains of living animals and algae, whether finely ground or coarse. Quartz is the most common mineral in sand because it is extremely hard-wearing and does not dissolve as other minerals do. However, most sandy beaches in the UK will be made of a mixture of both biogenic and mineral particles.

Very rarely a beach is known for emitting a sound when walked on – these have become known as whistling beaches although the sound is more usually a squeak. The theory behind this is that the grains of sand are almost purely quartz of a particular shape and size. As the dry grains rub against one another under pressure they emit a squeaking sound.

Sandy beach; on close inspection shell fragments may be apparent

Rocky or boulder beaches

Rocky beaches are those where the main component is bedrock, although patches of sand or pebbles may collect towards the back and between outcrops. Boulder beaches are constructed of large, often rounded rocks. The strandlines on these beaches tend to be patchy, and items collect in hollows and corners sheltered from the waves.

On this rocky beach, the limestone boulders have fallen as the cliff erodes

Shingle beaches

Shingle or pebble beaches can be among the longest beaches in the UK and can be very atmospheric places, with a wild, desolate feel to them. Shingle is a harsh environment for wildlife as any nutrients and freshwater rapidly drain through the gaps between the pebbles. However, a specialist wildlife community has found ways to overcome the disadvantages of shingle and make it their home. Pioneer plants send long roots down to find pockets of organic material buried deep under the pebbles, which soak up rainwater like a sponge. Lichens also grow on the surface, spreading and sticking the pebbles together. In this way the seaward edge of the shingle beach stabilises and new material thrown up by the sea is deposited in front, ready to start the process again. Shingle beaches often develop in a series of ridges with the most seaward ones colonised by pioneer plants and the more stable ones behind showing a succession of progressively more generalist plants.

Shingle beaches can be either natural or man-made for sea defence. Natural shingle beaches have rounder, more sea-worn pebbles

Maerl beaches

Maerl beaches are perhaps the rarest and are sometimes called coral beaches in the UK, although the material they are made of is not coral but a calcified alga. These beaches are made of dead nodules of Maerl that has lost its pink pigment, leaving just the white chalky framework of the plant (see page 46).

The best examples of Maerl beaches are to be found in north-west Scotland

Seaweeds

Seaweeds are the main component of the strandline. They end up on the beach after becoming detached from the seabed or being broken up in storms, or as a result of seasonal die-back. Once stranded out of water on a beach they quickly die and release nutrients, providing the base of the whole strandline ecosystem. The breakdown tends to be rapid as bacteria and detritivores such as Sand Hoppers and seaweed flies set to work, speeded up by heat from the sun and the composting process. Seaweeds act as a source of nutrients and a retainer of freshwater for beach plants, and on sandy beaches enable the process of dune formation to begin (see page 285).

On a few sandy beaches the strandline is dominated by eelgrass (a type of seagrass), which is not a seaweed but a marine flowering plant related to the more familiar plants we see on land. Eelgrass has an extensive root system and produces flowers and seeds which are dispersed by the sea. It grows in shallow, sandy areas where the roots penetrate the sand and bind it together to form a stable mat on the seabed. In winter, when it is not growing, it loses some of its grassy blades, and these can pile up on the beach in enough quantity to create a strandline. The blades, unlike seaweeds, dry out and become papery. The strandline formed by eelgrass tends not to be as diverse as those formed by seaweeds.

Seaweeds are a type of algae, sometimes called macro-algae, and are distinct from plants although they use pigments in their cells to trap energy from sunlight in a process called photosynthesis, in the same way as plants. However, the structure of a seaweed

FILTERING LIGHT

On land, most plants have green leaves for absorbing energy from sunlight. Their colour comes from the pigment inside, which traps the energy and converts it for use by the plant. Different types of pigment can trap different wavelengths of light, for example red or blue light. As light penetrates seawater, some wavelengths are filtered out in the first few metres while others penetrate much deeper.

For this reason different types of seaweed use a variety of pigments to trap light and appear in a much wider range of colours than land plants. Red and brown seaweeds mostly absorb blue-green light and can live at greater depths than green seaweeds, which mainly use red light and are most common in the shallower parts of the sea.

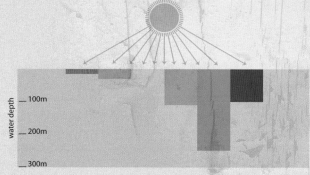

Depths to which different wavelengths of light can penetrate

Living seaweeds look very different to those stranded on the shore

is quite different, as it does not have roots to absorb water and nutrients, but instead absorbs them from the seawater it lives in through its outer surface. Some types of seaweed, such as kelp, have a structure with a holdfast (base), a stipe (stalk) and a frond or blade, while others may form flat sheets or spongy cushions or even balloon-like structures. The variety of seaweed shapes is enormous but almost all kinds need to be firmly attached to the seabed and have a holdfast for this purpose. They need to attach to a firm surface such as rock or man-made structures. Seaweeds tend to be grouped by their colour and are divided into red, brown and green seaweeds. The brown seaweeds are the dominant group on the seashore and include the kelps and wracks that are most familiar to us.

Six hundred and fifty different types of seaweed have been identified in the UK and in theory any of these could wash up onto a strandline. This section covers those species that commonly make up the strandline.

Seaweed as a host for other organisms

On a rocky seabed, attachment space is at a premium and some animals and algae take advantage of larger species to anchor themselves to. The large kelps can host a variety of 'hangers-on', from tiny Blue-rayed Limpets grazing on their fronds, to red seaweeds and hydroids attached to their tough stipe and a whole community of sponges, seasquirts, molluscs and crustaceans sheltering in their holdfast. When the host alga becomes detached its inhabitants suffer the same fate, left stranded on the beach to die.

Mechanical cleaning of beaches results in complete loss of strandline habitat

Seaweeds and people

Farming of seaweed is big business around the world where it is widely used in the cosmetics and food industry. It contains a variety of vitamins, calcium, iodine and protein, all of which are essential to our health. Historically, seaweeds washed up on beaches have been applied as fertiliser in agriculture. Some seaweeds can be used to clean polluted water as they grow quickly, absorbing excess nitrogen and phosphorus, and can then be harvested, removing the unwanted nutrients from the water.

When seaweed washes ashore in large quantities it can be regarded as a nuisance, especially on tourist beaches in the summer months. The problems associated with it include the smell as it decomposes, the associated flies that help break it down, and its slimy texture when you walk on it. This, along with its load of man-made litter, often results in mechanical removal of the whole strandline, providing a convenient short-term solution to the problem but resulting in a wildlife-barren beach and loss of an essential source of nutrients and stability to the coastline.

The tractor marks and lack of strandline indicate that this beach has been mechanically cleaned

27

Brown seaweeds

This group includes the largest and most complex seaweeds and in the UK is the dominant type of seaweed found on the shore. The colour, when fresh, varies from golden brown, olive green and even blue to deep brown, but when found on the strandline it may appear yellow, black or green as the pigment breaks down.

Kelps

In the UK this group contains the largest of all our seaweeds, which grow from the lowest part of the shore to a few metres depth in the sea. Being bulky seaweeds and subject to wave action, they are mostly tough and leathery to withstand being thrashed by waves. Their holdfast is often substantial as it needs to anchor them firmly to the seabed, even in stormy seas, while the blades tend to be smooth and rubbery in texture. They contain gummy chemicals to deter herbivores and these are released as the kelp decomposes on the strandline, giving them a slimy feel. Long after the main fronds of the seaweed have decomposed the more persistent parts, the holdfast and stipe, remain.

Furbelows holdfast

Cuvie holdfast

Dried kelp stipe

Furbelows *Saccorhiza polyschides*

Size 4m

Probably the bulkiest of our British kelps, with a distinctive warty, bulbous, hollow holdfast that is often found on strandlines. The long, strap-like blades emerge from a smooth, flattened stipe which is twisted at the bottom.

WHATEVER THE WEATHER

Sugar Kelp is also known as Poor Man's Weather Glass, as it is used to forecast the weather. Collect a fresh piece of Sugar Kelp from the strandline, rinse in seawater and take home. Dry it out by hanging somewhere sheltered but not heated. Once dried out you can feel it to predict the weather for that day – if it feels dry and crispy the weather should be fine, but if it's soft and flexible take your umbrella out with you!

There is some science behind the folklore – kelp is able to absorb moisture from the air so if rain is due, the moisture in the air gives the kelp a softer feel.

Sugar Kelp *Saccharina latissima*

Size 4m

Sometimes known as Sea Belt, this is a very distinctive seaweed consisting of a single long frond with a ruffled, wavy appearance, a short, smooth stipe and a claw-like holdfast.

Dabberlocks *Alaria esculenta*

Size 1.5m

This kelp grows on extremely wave-exposed coasts and resembles the single long frond of Sugar Kelp with crinkly edges, but with a tough mid-rib running the length of the frond. It could also be mistaken for Wakame if not complete. However, the reproductive parts are distinctive, consisting of a bunch of long fingers attached below the frond.

Oar Weed *Laminaria digitata*

Size 2m

This kelp is distinguished from others by its hand-like blade, smooth, flexible stipe and branched holdfast. An alternative name is Smooth-stalked Kelp. The strap-like fingers of the blade gradually shred and are worn away in winter storms with new growth starting from the palm-like base of the blade in spring.

Cuvie *Laminaria hyperborea*

Size 3.5m

This type of kelp can be confused with Oar Weed but instead of the smooth stipe it has a rough surface, which is often overgrown by other seaweeds and hydroids. Its alternative name is Rough-stalked Kelp.

OAR WEED OR CUVIE?

Apart from their different stipe texture there is a simple way to tell Oar Weed and Cuvie apart.

Bend the stipe as far as possible – if it bends without breaking it is Oar Weed, if it snaps when bent it is Cuvie!

Oar Weed

Cuvie

Oar Weed with its smooth, clean stipe (below) and Cuvie with its rougher textured stipe (above)

Wakame *Undaria pinnatifida*

Size 2m

Also called Asian Kelp, this is not a native seaweed but was introduced into Europe for farming and was first recorded in the UK in the 1990s on the Channel coast. It could be confused with Furbelows but has some distinctive features. The frond emerges horizontally from a midrib and is divided into straps. The branched holdfast distinguishes it immediately from Furbelows. The reproductive structures on this seaweed consist of a number of folds at the base of the short stipe, reminiscent of an Elizabethan ruff.

Mermaid's Tresses *Chorda filum*

Size 8m

Also commonly known as Bootlace Weed, this seaweed is very distinctive, consisting of a single, unbranched, bootlace-like frond. In life it is a long, hollow, cylindrical tube covered in fine hairs, giving it a fuzzy appearance underwater. On the strandline it looks like long bundles of spaghetti. It grows in sheltered locations.

Wracks

Wracks are a family of brown seaweeds that dominate the intertidal zone on British shores. They are arranged along the shore in zones, depending on how well adapted they are to surviving out of water while the tide is out. Those living highest on the shore, furthest from the sea at low tide, are able to survive for several days out of water and make the most of the short time when the tide is high enough to cover them up. Those living in the middle of the shore spend half the time in and half out of water, while those living lower on the shore are only able to spend a short time exposed to the air. Living in this rapidly changing environment, these seaweeds need to be firmly anchored but exposure to breaking waves means that they can be torn off the rocks and thrown onto the strandline. The larger species are more vulnerable to this. There are a number of different types of wrack to be found around the coast – the most commonly found species are described here.

Egg Wrack *Ascophyllum nodosum*

Size 1.5m

Egg Wrack, also known as Knotted Wrack, is a bulky mid-shore seaweed which is identified by its row of large single air bladders along the frond. When fresh it is olive-green in colour (inset), but when dried out on the strandline it can appear almost black (main photo).

This is a relatively long-lived seaweed, the stipe growing a single new air bladder along its length each year. Being large and bulky, it is particularly vulnerable to damage by waves and grows best on sheltered seashores where it can dominate the shore and the strandline.

Egg Wrack with goose barnacles attached can sometimes be found on the strandline. This has drifted across the Atlantic ocean from North America, remaining alive as it floats, buoyed up by its air bladders, on the surface of the sea. It often appears quite yellow in colour and as well as goose barnacles it may have hydroids and sea mat attached to its surface.

Bladder Wrack *Fucus vesiculosus*

Size 90cm

Bladder Wrack is a bulky mid-shore seaweed commonly found on the strandline. It is easily distinguished from Egg Wrack as it has pairs of small, blister-like air bladders arranged along the frond, as opposed to single, large ones. The air bladders are a device used by the alga to help it stand upright underwater, as it needs to receive the maximum amount of sunlight for photosynthesis.

Serrated Wrack *Fucus serratus*

Size 60cm

Also known as Toothed Wrack, this seaweed has a serrated, saw-like edge to the frond and a distinct midrib as found in a leaf. It is found on the lower shore, where it is not exposed to the air for too long when the tide is out. Being underwater for most of the time it provides an opportunity for marine animals to attach and is often encrusted with the tiny coiled tubes of the tube worm *Spirorbis spirorbis*. When washed onto the strandline the worms will die but their 3–4mm chalky white tubes remain attached to the surface of the weed.

SEA WHISTLES

The egg-shaped air bladders of Egg Wrack can measure up to 5cm long and when dried out are very hard. They persist in the strandline long after the rest of the seaweed has disappeared and can be used to make whistles. This has given the alga the alternative names of Whistle Weed and Sea Whistle.

Take a single large, dried and hardened air bladder and scrape a slit into the top. By blowing across the slit you should be able to produce a musical note.

Channelled Wrack *Pelvetia canaliculata*

Size 15cm

This is a short, brown seaweed growing high in the intertidal zone. Its frond is curled, forming a channel to retain moisture when exposed at low tide. This is an adaptation that allows it to spend long periods out of water, when it can appear dried and crispy, but it has the ability to rapidly absorb seawater when the tide returns.

Rainbow Wrack *Cystoseira tamariscifolia*

Size 45cm

This bushy, brown seaweed with tough main stems is notable for its colour-changing ability. Although it looks brown when out of water or on the strandline, underwater it appears to be a variety of shades of blue, from pale turquoise to deep violet. A fresh piece, if returned to the water, will instantly change to blue – giving rise to its alternative name of Magic Seaweed.

Thongweed *Himanthalia elongata*

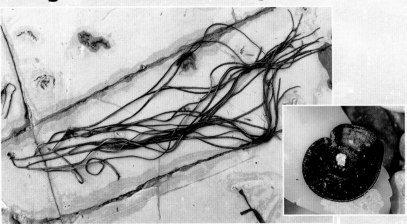

Size 2m

This seaweed consists of a small, mushroom-shaped 'button', which is the main body of the alga, and long, forked straps, which are the reproductive parts. It grows on open coasts where, once its reproductive cycle is complete, it is vulnerable to being torn up by waves and ending up on the strandline. Often just the straps are found on the strandline but sometimes the whole specimen, complete with its brown, leathery button, is found.

Wireweed *Sargassum muticum*

Size 2m

This is a highly invasive, non-native seaweed that first arrived on the south coast of England in the 1970s. It is native to the Pacific Ocean, hence its alternative name of Japanese Seaweed. It grows in sheltered locations and rockpools. In life it is golden-brown in colour, growing in dense stands, but when washed up it can look very dark brown. It is long and bushy with many tiny, oval blades and small spherical air bladders. An easy way to identify it is to hold a strand horizontally – the branches will hang down from the main stem, like washing on a line.

Sea Oak *Halidrys siliquosa*

Size 2m

Also known as Pod Weed, this large seaweed is much-branched and flattened and has characteristic flattened and ridged air bladders or pods. These sometimes become separated from the plant and can be found in piles on the strandline. The seaweed itself can make up a substantial part of the strandline, being common and bulky.

Sargasso weed *Sargassum fluitans* & *S. natans*

S. fluitans

Size Raft-forming

Sargasso weed, also known as Gulf weed, has evolved without a holdfast to attach it to the seabed and instead is designed to float in large rafts on the slowly rotating water of the Sargasso Sea which was named after the weed itself. The two species of Sargasso weed are the world's only free-floating, large algae. Although there are only anecdotal records of these species stranding on UK beaches, beachcombers should look out for them. The two species, when stranded, are brown with many tiny leaflets and air bladders and lacking a holdfast,

S. natans

possibly in a wreath formation. *Sargassum fluitans* has broad leaflets and no spike on the round air bladders, whereas *Sargassum natans* has narrow leaflets and a spike on the end of each bladder. It is distinguished from the more familiar *Sargassum muticum* (above) which is linear in shape with a small holdfast.

THE SARGASSO SEA

The Sargasso Sea lies at the centre of an ocean gyre, with currents circulating around its edges and the island of Bermuda at its heart. The rafts of floating, golden Sargasso weed provide a very important and unique habitat for some unusual and specialised marine species. The seabed ranges from the shallow coral reefs of Bermuda to the deep ocean at some 4,500m. The animals that live there are associated with the extensive mats of floating Sargasso weed, whether they live on, in or underneath it.

It is probable that the Columbus Crabs, *Planes minutus*, (also known as Gulf Weed Crabs) that wash up on UK beaches originate from the Sargasso Sea and it is highly possible that chunks of Sargasso weed, along with their inhabitants, break off from time to time and are carried by the Gulf Stream across the Atlantic. It is worth looking out for some species that have not so far been recorded in the UK, particularly the nudibranch, *Scyllaea pelagica*, known as the Sargasso Nudibranch, which is green and brown in colour, with white patches to blend in with the Sargasso weed on which it lives.

Sargasso Nudibranch, *Scyllaea pelagica*

Other brown seaweeds

Oyster Thief *Colpomenia peregrina*

Size 7cm

This seaweed forms a hollow, air-filled, golden-brown sphere and when washed onto the beach is often mistaken for an egg of some sort. The sphere is thin-walled and quite papery, being easily torn. It is a non-native seaweed first recorded in England in 1907 and grows attached to seaweed, rocks and shells on the seabed. It can be a pest in oyster farms as, if it grows large enough, it can float away with its oyster host – hence its English name.

Green seaweeds

Although this group is relatively small, some intertidal species can appear in abundance on seashores and a couple of species are fairly commonly found on the strandline. They can often be quick-growing, colonising areas that are unsuitable for longer-lived algae, but completing their lifecycle and disappearing before conditions become too harsh. For this reason they may be found on seashores where there is a lot of freshwater, or may indicate sewage or pollution input. However, they are not necessarily an indicator of this and may just be a natural part of the seashore community.

Sea Lettuce *Ulva lactuca*

Size 30cm

As the name suggests, this lettuce-like seaweed consists of an emerald green, flattened, wavy-edged frond. The frond is membranous and almost translucent with a smooth texture. In very sheltered estuaries it can grow into extensive sheets floating on the surface, which under certain conditions can be deposited onto beaches. Once washed ashore it rapidly bleaches as the pigment breaks down and can look like a pile of soggy tissues.

Gutweed *Ulva intestinalis*

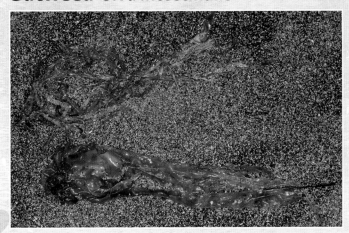

Size Up to 75cm

A bright green seaweed consisting of thin hollow tubes which in life would be filled with oxygen produced by the plant. As it can cope with brackish water it grows in estuaries, upper shore rockpools or where there is a freshwater stream or run-off on the beach. It can often be found growing on fishing buoys and other drifting objects, or as strands or clumps stranded on the beach. Gutweed belongs to a large group of very similar and closely related species.

Velvet Horn *Codium tomentosum*

Size 30cm

This seaweed comes from a very confusing group, several of which can be found on British strandlines. Velvet Horn is a native seaweed but the more commonly found Green Sea Fingers, *Codium fragile*, is a non-native that looks very similar but is larger, possibly growing to around 1m in length. However, they have the same overall appearance, being dark green and bushy, and made up of branched, spongy fingers with a velvety texture and rounded tips.

Rock Weed *Cladophora rupestris*

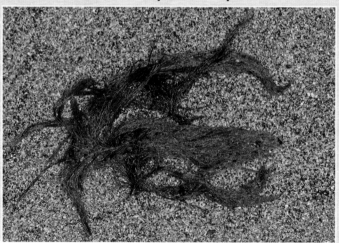

Size 20cm

This is a dark bluish-green, feathery seaweed with numerous fine branches, which grows in the middle shore. Despite its fine, feathery structure it feels quite coarse in texture.

SEAWEED PRESSING

Seaweed pressing is a great activity to do after a visit to the beach. You can make stunning pictures or build up your own personal catalogue of the different species, complete with memories of where and when you collected them. You will need:

- shallow tray
- sheet of plain paper
- fine paint brush
- nappy liner or absorbent, reusable cleaning cloth
- newspapers

Then follow these simple steps.

1. Pour a little tap water into your tray – enough to cover the bottom. Then slide your sheet of paper into the water so the water covers it.
2. After rinsing the sand off your seaweed, arrange it on top of the paper in the water. Use the fine paintbrush to arrange the fronds so they don't clump together.
3. Gently slide the paper out of the water. As the paper emerges the seaweed should stick to it but you need to be slow and careful.
4. Now place your paper on a few sheets of newspaper
5. Place a nappy liner or reusable cleaning cloth on top of the seaweed to stop the newspaper sticking to it. Cover with another layer of newspaper.
6. Put the whole lot underneath a pile of heavy books and leave somewhere to dry out.

You will need to replace the wet newspaper with dry every day or two to prevent mould. After a few days your seaweed should be dry and pressed, and ready to frame or add to your catalogue. Don't forget to add a note to say what it is and where and when you collected it.

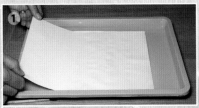

Red seaweeds

This is the biggest and most diverse group of seaweeds. Fossil records show that red seaweeds were around 1.2 billion years ago, making them the oldest known seaweed group on Earth. Colour and form are highly variable, ranging from scarlet or pink to maroon and almost black in colour, while structure can include delicate films, fine and feathery, encrusting and even articulated forms.

There are around 6,500 species worldwide including 350 species in the UK alone. Below are described the most commonly found types that appear on strandlines.

Maerl *Phymatolithon calcareum*

Size 6cm

So-called 'coral beaches' in the UK are formed entirely of dead Maerl that has been washed up from the seabed (see page 23). Underwater, Maerl forms extensive beds and is recognised as an important marine habitat, supporting a very particular wildlife community. Maerl beds are actually made up of several different species of alga. Individual pieces or specimens are pink in colour and contain calcium carbonate in their structure, which gives them a coral-like appearance. Maerl forms irregular, branching nodules which are not attached but interlock to carpet the sea floor in beds that can be several metres deep. On the beach it loses its coloration and turns orange or white.

Coral Weed *Corallina officinalis*

Size 7cm

This is an erect, feather-shaped, branched seaweed, pink in colour and containing a 'skeleton' of calcium carbonate. It is commonly found in low-shore rockpools. On the strandline it loses its coloration, leaving just a white, jointed chain of chalky segments.

Jania rubens (below) is smaller, growing to just 2.5cm, and is a more delicate type of calcareous seaweed which might be mistaken for Coral Weed. However, it is less common and tends to form balls rather than feather-shaped fronds.

Jania rubens

Clawed Fork Weed *Furcellaria lumbricalis*

Size 30cm
This bushy, red seaweed is formed of many long, fleshy, cylindrical fronds which fork and have tapered tips, giving it a spiky appearance. The red colour often fades to brown with yellow or green tips when stranded. The lower sections are sometimes encrusted with spiral worm tubes.

Red Sea Pine *Halopithys incurva*

Size 20cm
A bushy, dark red seaweed which is wiry in texture and often fouled with other organisms such as purse sponges and spiral worms. On the strandline it darkens in colour and can look almost black. It is a southern species.

Fine-veined Crinkle Weed *Cryptopleura ramosa*

Size 20cm

This red seaweed consists of long, thin, crinkly-edged fronds, resembling ribbons. When fresh it appears smooth and shiny, while underwater it exhibits a blue iridescence.

Sea Beech *Delesseria sanguinea*

Size 25cm

As the name suggests, the fronds of this seaweed resemble the leaves of a beech tree but are scarlet in colour. They have a thick mid-rib with fine veins branching off, and a filmy membrane between. The mid-rib, which often fades to pink, remains intact after the filmy frond has begun to disintegrate.

Irish Moss *Chondrus crispus*

Size 22cm

Irish Moss, or Carrageen, is a common seaweed all around the UK coastline. Although it is very variable in form, its basic shape is fan-shaped with fronds that divide, or fork, at intervals. It can range from deep purplish-red, sometimes with iridescent tips, to green, yellow or even white when bleached.

This seaweed contains carrageenan, an extract which has been used in foods and medicines since the early 19th century. Carrageenan has a number of useful properties, including as a gelling agent, making it a vegetarian alternative to gelatine. It is also used as an emulsifier, thickener or stabiliser in toothpaste, shampoo and paint and in food products such as non-dairy milks and ice-cream. It is even used to clarify beer.

SEAWEED JELLY

To extract carrageenan and see its gelling properties for yourself, take home a bunch of freshly washed up Irish Moss and put it in a pan on the stove. Cover with a little water, bring to the boil and then turn off the heat. When the water cools it will have turned gelatinous. This is the carrageenan coming out of the weed and is why this seaweed is used extensively in the food industry as a thickener and gelling agent.

Northern Tooth Weed *Odonthalia dentata*

Size 30cm

This red seaweed is a northern species. Its flat fronds, which are about 1cm wide, have a serrated or toothed edge and a thin mid-rib, making it quite easy to identify.

Red Rags *Dilsea carnosa*

Size 50cm

This red seaweed grows in flat, wide, irregular sheets that are slightly longer than wide. It has a tough but smooth texture and on the strandline may appear torn and tatty with holes appearing in the frond.

Eyelash Weed *Calliblepharis ciliata*

Size 30cm

This red seaweed grows from a small, branched holdfast with a very short, thin stipe. The broad, flat blade has many fine outgrowths along the edges, giving it a frilly appearance. Unlike Red Rags which might appear similar, the texture of the frond is coarse rather than smooth.

Dulse *Palmaria palmata*

Size 50cm

Sometimes called Dillisk in Ireland, this leafy, deep-red seaweed is often found on the strandline attached to the stipes of Cuvie (see page 32). The flat fronds divide and often have tiny leaflets growing along their margins, giving them an irregular growth pattern. Dulse is one of the few seaweeds traditionally eaten uncooked (carefully and rapidly dried) and if prepared properly can have a pleasant taste. Regulations for gathering this species are mentioned in the Icelandic sagas of the 10th century.

Eelgrass *Zostera* spp.

Seagrasses are one of very few types of flowering plant that live in the sea, and can form extensive meadows on the seabed in shallow water. In the UK, the type of seagrass we find is called eelgrass. Eelgrass is different from seaweed as it has roots and produces seeds. It grows in shallow, sheltered, sunlit waters on sandy seabeds where its roots penetrate, forming a thick mat beneath the surface that binds the loose sand together.

The leaves, looking like tall grass, can measure over 1m in length, and form a dense covering on the sea floor, creating an ideal shelter for many species. It is recognised as an important habitat for juvenile fish and provides a vital nursery area for many commercial species. Flatfish such as plaice and sole are found here, as are bass, bream, pollock and even rays. It is also known as the preferred habitat for many species of seahorse around the world.

Dried eelgrass

Eelgrass meadows provide a natural coastal defence, absorbing the energy from waves before they reach the shore. Eelgrass is also recognised as an important 'blue carbon sink', capturing carbon dioxide from the seawater and locking it away inside its cells. In this way it helps in the fight against climate change.

Freshly stranded eelgrass

As seagrass grows in sheltered bays and estuaries, it often comes under pressure from human activities. Much has been lost around the world as a result of coastal development, such as building marinas and hard sea defences, fishing, pollution and anchoring. In the 1930s a wasting disease wiped out many eelgrass meadows in the UK. Now it is internationally recognised as an important habitat, acting like an oasis and providing food and shelter for a myriad of animals on an otherwise featureless seabed. Much of the marine life living there is specialised for this habitat, evolved for camouflage in the grassy leaves.

Eelgrass grows in spring and summer, when sunlight is strongest, and dies back a little in winter, when some of the leaves turn brown and break off, washing up on adjacent beaches. Its leaves form an unusual strandline, the dead leaves drying and turning papery when washed ashore. Successive tides can push this strandline up the beach, forming folds as each new deposit is added at the seaward side. Eventually the material will be buried in wind-blown sand, where it acts like an underground 'grow-bag' for pioneer dune plants. As this fore dune is formed it protects the dunes behind from erosion. On beaches that are mechanically cleaned this material is removed, halting the natural process of dune formation and potentially causing the acceleration of coastal erosion.

Folds of stranded eelgrass

Shells

S hells are often among the most numerous items making up the strandline and tell us a lot about the animals living in the local marine environment. In some cases broken shells are a major component of the beach itself. The strandline is therefore a good place to get to know and recognise the different species of marine molluscs living around our coastline.

There are two major groups of mollusc that produce a protective shell – the gastropod, which produces a single shell, often spiral in form, and the bivalve, which has a hinged shell in two parts. Almost all of the shells you find on the strandline will be from these two groups.

Different beaches will have their own assortment of shells to find. A beach adjacent to a sandy seabed will collect mostly the shells of bivalve molluscs that burrow into the sand, whereas a rocky shore will accumulate the shells of gastropods, crawling seasnails living on the hard seabed or on the seaweed attached to it.

As well as identifying the animal the shell belonged to, also check for signs of predation. Some marine snails prey on other molluscs by boring through their hard shell. Look for small, perfectly round holes drilled through limpet, mussel and other rocky shore mollusc shells – this is evidence of predation by Dog Whelks or Sting Winkles (see page 80). On sandy shores, bivalve shells sometimes sport a similar perfectly round hole bored close to the hinge joining the two halves (valves). This is evidence of predation by Necklace Shells (see page 72).

Limpet shell exhibiting predation by Dog Whelk

This section covers the most common shells found on strandlines. If you wish to delve deeper into the marine mollusc world, consider investing in a seashore book or one dedicated to sea shells.

With an absence of seaweeds, the shells here define the strandline

Sandy shore

Bivalves

Shells found on sandy shores, with a sandy seabed offshore, are predominantly from bivalve molluscs. Sandy seabeds, with no hard surfaces for seaweed to attach, are flat, open, underwater plains with nowhere for an animal to hide from predators, therefore most of the molluscs that live there are buried beneath the surface. Rather than crawling around to find food, they wait for the sea to bring it to them. These animals extend a tube or siphon to the surface of the sand to extract nutrients, either from the seawater or from the detritus settling on the seabed. When they sense danger they instantly retract their siphon, disappearing beneath the surface. At low tide you can observe this while walking across the sands, as rapid retraction of siphons results in jets of water squirting out.

Bivalve siphons

Some bivalves, such as scallops, live at the surface of the sand and do not burrow. Whilst unable to crawl, they can move around by clapping the two halves of their shell together. This limited ability to swim enables them to escape from slow-moving predators such as starfish, and also to find the best locations for feeding. They allow their shell valves to gape open to draw in a flow of seawater, from which they extract food.

The sensory tentacles and eyes can be easily seen on this live scallop

Common Oyster *Ostrea edulis*

Size 11cm

As a result of its historic abundance and more recent over-exploitation, many of the Common Oyster shells found on beaches are the remains of long-dead animals. Fresh shells are circular or oval, off-white on the rough, scaly outside and pearly on the smooth inside.

Saddle Oyster *Anomia ephippium*

Size 5cm

This is a thin, rounded shell in which one of the two shell valves has an oval hole near the hinge, through which it attaches to substrate using fine byssal threads.

Pod Razor Shell *Ensis siliqua*

Size 20cm

The largest of several species of razor shell found on strandlines. Its long, rectangular shape resembles an old-fashioned cut-throat razor. The outer surface of these brittle shells has a flaky coating (periostracum) and it is often found with both valves still attached.

Common Razor Shell *Ensis ensis*

Size 12cm

This type of razor shell has a slightly curved shape. It is a more delicate shell than the Pod Razor Shell.

Grooved Razor Shell *Solen marginatus*

Size 12cm

The Grooved Razor Shell is wider than the Common Razor Shell and straight-sided. Both valves of the shell have a distinctive groove at one end.

Pharus legumen

Size 12cm

This animal is similar to razor shells, with an elongated shell. Both ends are rounded with one end tapering and the hinge is in the middle of one long edge, rather than running the whole length as it does in the razor shells.

Blunt Gaper *Mya truncata*

Size 7cm

A robust, creamy coloured shell with a slightly rectangular shape, being squared off at one end. This end gapes open when the two shell-valves are closed.

Piddocks Pholadidae

Four species of piddock can be found on beach strandlines and all have white shells. They are elongated with an offset, rather than central, hinge. The end nearest the hinge has a series of rough ridges, which the animal uses for drilling into hard substrates.

Common Piddock *Pholas dactylus*

Size 14cm

White Piddock *Barnea candida*

Size 6cm

Oval Piddock *Zirfaea crispata*

Size 9cm

American Piddock *Petricola pholadiformis*

Size 8cm

BORING PIDDOCKS

Piddocks are boring bivalves with pronounced ridges at one end of their shell, to enable them to burrow into soft rock, wood and clay. As a piddock rotates its shell, the ridges drill deep into the substrate, creating a protective burrow in which the mollusc lives, extending feeding siphons out into the water. As the rock erodes, pieces or chunks can be found with the distinctive round boring holes of the piddock, sometimes with

Piddock holes in rock

sections of burrow complete with the shells still wedged inside. The siphons of the Common Piddock are phosphorescent, glowing green in the dark.

This feeding siphon gives away the presence of a buried piddock

Common Cockle *Cerastoderma edule*

Size 4.5cm

The most commonly found of several types of cockle. Deep-bodied, rounded and oval in shape, it is often found with both valves still attached. The shells are ridged and thick.

Dog Cockle *Glycymeris glycymeris*

Size 6cm

Smooth, rounded, shell, patterned with brown zig-zag lines on a creamy background. Concentric growth lines are visible.

Norway Cockle *Laevicardium crassum*

Size 7cm
Rounded shell with narrow, shallow ridges radiating from the hinge. The cream-coloured shell usually retains some of the brown flaky periostracum, giving it a patchy, worn appearance.

Spiny, Prickly and Rough Cockles
Acanthocardia aculeata, A. echinata, A. tuberculata

Size 9.5cm
These thick, ridged, deep-bodied shells, are normally found with spines along the ridges, although these may be worn down, with the most pronounced spines towards the outer edge of the shell. The three species are very similar, and once washed up and worn can be very difficult to distinguish. Some beaches may have shells from more than one of these species on the strandline.

Variegated Scallop *Chalamys varia*

Size 6cm

This scallop has a slightly elongated oval shell with fine ridges, often with spines along them which may be worn away. One hinge-wing is much larger than the other. Colour varies but is usually dark orange to purple, although they often become bleached on the strandline. Note the holes bored by predatory snails in this photo (see page 80).

Otter Shell *Lutraria lutraria*

Size 15cm

A large, oval, off-white shell, often found with both valves still attached. Fresh shells still have a brownish coating on the outside, which wears away.

Icelandic Cyprine *Arctica islandica*

Size 11cm

A large, round, deep-bodied shell, with a dark brown periostracum. The Icelandic Cyprine is one of the longest living of all animals and can survive for several hundred years. One has been recorded living for more than 500 years. It is amazing to think that the shell you find may be from an animal that was alive when Shakespeare was writing Romeo and Juliet, and Queen Elizabeth I was on the throne!

Pullet Carpet Shell *Venerupis corrugata*

Size 5cm

A pale, roughly oval shell. The outside has a series of fine rings or grooves, sometimes with faint brown markings. There are a number of species of carpet shell, all with the same basic shape, but they can be difficult to identify when bleached and worn on the strandline.

Thick Trough Shell *Spisula solida*

Size 5cm

A pale shell with yellowish, concentric rings and a roughly triangular shape with a curved outer edge. As the name suggests, this is a thick, robust shell which usually survives intact.

Rayed Trough Shell *Mactra stultorum*

Size 5cm

A thin, fragile shell, usually with a pinkish tinge and very smooth inner surface. The shell displays pale concentric growth rings and also has darker lines radiating out from the hinge. It is roughly triangular with a curved outer edge.

Warty Venus *Venus verrucosa*

Size 6cm

A thick, creamy grey shell with obvious concentric ridges which have bumps on them, giving the warty appearance. These become more exaggerated towards the outer edge of the shell.

Striped Venus *Chamelea gallina*

Size 4cm

A glossy, roughly triangular shell with brown coloured concentric ridges on a pale background. Two pale lines radiate out from the curved hinge, dividing each valve into three broad, brown bands.

Tellins Tellinidae

Size Up to 2.6cm

There are several species of tellin that could be found on UK strandlines, of which the most common are, the Thin Tellin, *Tellinus tenuis,* and the Baltic Tellin, *Macoma balthica*. These species both have thin, delicate shells, which burrow beneath sand on the lower shore, sometimes in huge numbers. Both species grow to around 26mm and, although colour can be variable they often have a pinkish tinge, especially the Thin Tellin. Shape is roughly oval and the Thin Tellin is slightly flatter than the Baltic Tellin.

Banded Wedge Shell *Donax vittatus*

Size 3.5cm

This is a thin, roughly oval and gently wedge-shaped shell. Colour can vary from yellow or orange to pink or purple with darker bands and a shiny outer surface. The very fine ridges along the inner surface of the outer edge can be felt by running a fingernail along it. Banded Wedge Shells are often found with tellins.

Gastropods

Slipper Limpet *Crepidula fornicata*

Size 5cm

This non-native mollusc was introduced from North America, and now is locally abundant in the southern half of the UK. The pinkish, oval shell has a white shelf extending over half of the underside. Live animals are often washed up attached to other shells, or to each other in stacks of up to 12 animals.

HIGH-RISE LIVING

Slipper Limpets form stacks or chains with the largest, the only female, at the bottom, and the animals stacked above gradually reducing in size to the smallest male at the top. When the female dies the largest male, at the bottom of the chain becomes a female.

Necklace Shell *Euspira catena*

Size 3cm

A smooth, globular, bluntly spiral shell, buff-coloured and often found broken. This predator of bivalve molluscs drills a hole through the shells of its prey to access the flesh inside. In spring it produces 'egg collars' made of sand bound in a jelly-like substance (see page 95).

A close relative, the **Alder's Necklace Shell**, *Euspira pulchella*, is very similar but smaller at just 1.5cm high.

Turban Top Shell *Gibbula magus*

Size 3cm

A conical, flattened, spiral shell with a stepped profile and pink diagonal stripes. Most other types of top shell are found on rocky shores.

Pelican's Foot *Aporrhais pespelecani*

Size 4.2cm

A distinctive and attractive spiral shell with the edge fanning out to resemble a water bird's webbed foot. It lives just beneath the surface of muddy sand, the animal using the shape of its shell to forge a path through the sediment.

Auger Shell *Turritella communis*

Size 5.5cm

A distinctive, elongated spiral shell with a sharp tip. This shell is usually pale brown in colour but this can fade on the strandline. In life, Auger Shells are buried beneath the surface of the sand.

Common Whelk *Buccinum undatum*

Size 11cm

The iconic seashell used by children to listen to the sea. It is also commonly inhabited by hermit crabs after the snail's death. It is a large, spiral, pale coloured shell. Common Whelks lay spongy egg-masses called 'seawash balls' often found on strandlines (see page 95).

The **Red Whelk,** *Neptunea antiqua* (inset), can be larger at up to 20cm long, with a smooth shell and a narrower aperture, tapering towards the tip. It is mainly found on northern coasts.

Netted Dog Whelk *Hinia reticulata*

Size 3cm

A small, brown, spiral shell with chequered markings. These scavengers live beneath the sandy seabed from where they erupt *en masse* to feed on dead fish, crabs or other animals (inset). The empty shells are often inhabited by hermit crabs.

Rocky shore

Gastropods

The shells found on rocky shores are predominantly from gastropods, single-shelled molluscs. These animals crawl around on the surface of the seabed and amongst seaweed, using their toothed radula to feed.

Common Limpet *Patella vulgata*

Size 6cm

A conical, pale shell sometimes abundant on rocky shore strandlines. Common, Black-footed and China Limpet look very similar. Limpets are famous for their strong muscular foot that attaches them tightly to rocks at low tide.

Black-footed Limpet *Patella depressa*

Size 3cm

A conical shell, slightly flattened and with dark, quite pronounced rays around the edge of the inside. It does not grow as large as the Common Limpet.

China Limpet *Patella ulyssiponensis*

Size 5cm

A conical shell, the inside being glossy white tinged with an orangey centre.

LIMPET TRACKS

Limpets play a key role on rocky shores, where they feed by scraping the film of algal spores left behind on the rock after each tide. Like all gastropods, limpets have a radula, a toothed, ribbon-like tongue, and as they forage across the rocky seashore they leave zig-zag tracks made by scratching the rock. By clearing some areas of seaweed growth and creating a patchwork effect, they enable other animals to settle and increase the diversity of the seashore. The rasping of limpets and other gastropods can sometimes be heard, especially at night when the tide is out.

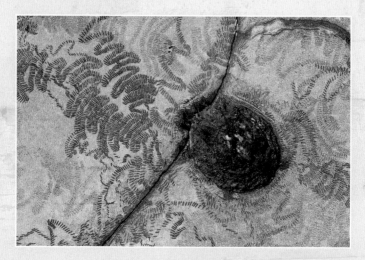

Blue-rayed Limpet *Helcion pellucidum*

Size 1.5cm
A small, conical shell with fine electric-blue radiating lines, which fade in large individuals or stranded shells. These snails live and feed on kelp fronds, sometimes overwintering in the holdfast, which is a good place to look for them on the strandline.

Common Periwinkle *Littorina littorea*

Size 3cm
A thick, black or dark brown spiral shell with a smooth outer surface.

Rough Periwinkle *Littorina saxatilis*

Size 1.7cm
Similar to the Common Periwinkle but more varied in colour and smaller, this shell has ridges running around the spiral outside of the shell.

Flat Periwinkle *Littorina obtusata*

Size 1cm

This shell comes in two main colour varieties, bright yellow, looking like a piece of sweetcorn, or dark brown. It is small and rounded with a blunt or flattened spire.

Flat Top Shell *Gibbula umbilicalis*

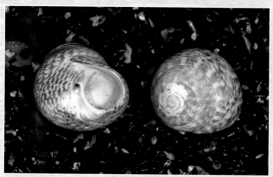

Size 2cm

A flattened spiral shell with pinkish purple candy-stripes, which often wears away to reveal a silvery mother-of-pearl layer beneath. It often has a visible hole running from top to underside through the centre of the spire.

Grey Top Shell *Gibbula cineraria*

Size 1.5cm
A rounded spiral shell, roughly triangular in outline, with very fine brown diagonal lines and no central hole.

Painted Top Shell *Calliostoma zizyphinum*

Size 3cm
A pretty shell with a sharply pointed apex, resembling an old-fashioned spinning top. Often pale with pinkish-brown markings and sometimes revealing a silvery mother-of-pearl layer.

Toothed Top Shell *Phorcus lineatus*

Size 3cm
A dark purple spiral shell with faint diagonal lines on top and white or silver beneath. It has a small bump (tooth) at the entrance to the aperture.

Dog Whelk *Nucella lapillus*

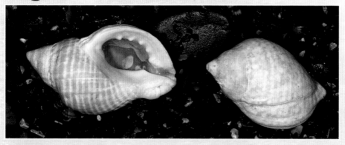

Size 4cm

A thick, pointed spiral shell which can vary in colour depending on its food. It is often creamy grey but can be orange-coloured or striped. The entrance (aperture) has a deep groove or channel.

European Sting Winkle *Ocenebra erinacea*

Size 5cm

This is similar to the Dog Whelk but with a very ridged spiral shell with a stepped profile.

DRILLER KILLER

Dog Whelks and European Sting Winkles are predatory molluscs which use their toothed radula to drill holes through the shells of other gastropods, softening them with a chemical to ease the process. Once they have penetrated the shell, they inject more chemicals to paralyse and digest their prey, liquidising it before sucking it out through the hole. Look for shells with tiny holes drilled through on the strandline.

A Dog Whelk predating a live limpet

Arctic Cowrie *Trivia arctica*

Size 1cm

Tiny, oval, ribbed shells, buff or pinkish-coloured. This animal has a plain shell, while its relative, the **Spotted Cowrie**, *Trivia monacha*, looks the same but with three dark spots on the top (centre of photo).

Bivalves

Common Mussel *Mytilus edulis*

Size 6cm

A fan-shaped shell, dark blue in colour and sometimes fading to silver at the tip. This bivalve mollusc uses fine strands called byssus threads to anchor it to rocks. The two valves of the shell are often found still attached to each other.

King Scallop *Pecten maximus*

Size 12cm
The classic scallop shell with a circular outline and ridges radiating from the hinge which has a an equal-sized pair of wings. It has an orange outside and a glossy white inside. One valve is flat while the other is curved.

Queen Scallop *Aequipecten opercularis*

Size 9cm
Similar but smaller than the King Scallop, this shell has two curved valves, more and narrower ridges and one hinge-wing larger than the other.

THE SOUND OF THE SEA

As children, many of us would have held a seashell to our ear to listen to the sound of the sea, even when far from the coast. There is something magical about the sound, but how is it produced?

The best shells to use for this are large, spiral shells such as whelks. When you hold the opening to your ear, especially on a breezy day, the external sound resonates inside the confines of the shell. Keep the shell to recapture the roar of the ocean, wherever you are.

Eggcases and eggs

L ots of marine animals produce eggs but only a small number are regularly found on the strandline. These include the mermaid's purses – empty outer casings of eggs laid by sharks, skates and rays, and egg-masses laid by other fish and invertebrates in shallow, inshore waters. Unhatched eggs wash ashore when they become detached from their seabed anchorage in rough weather, while empty eggcases become light, floating to the sea's surface, and are driven onshore by wind and waves.

Eggs and eggcases found on the beach give clues as to what is living just offshore. Some are seasonal and will only be found at certain times of year, depending on the breeding cycle of the animal in question.

Mermaid's purses

This delightful name refers to the tough, empty egg capsules of a variety of sharks, skates and rays and invokes memories of childhood, wandering along beach strandlines collecting these crisp, black and golden pouches, and imagining what they could be and where they came from. Sharks, skates and rays belong to the group of fish called

elasmobranchs and are different from bony fish in that instead of having a bony skeleton, theirs is made of cartilage. They differ in other ways too, one being that they produce relatively few offspring. Not all elasmobranchs lay eggs on the seabed, some produce eggs which hatch inside the mother, resulting in the birth of live young.

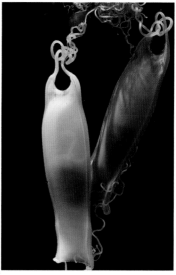

In the UK there are only a handful of species that lay eggs, anchoring them on the seabed or entwined around seaweed, sea fans and other static objects. Inside the tough outer casing of each individual egg is a nutritious yolk and a single developing embryo. When the embryo wriggles or pumps its tail inside the egg, this brings freshly oxygenated seawater in and pushes stale water out through the hollow 'horns' of the eggcase. Over several months the

Above: Small-spotted Catshark embryos developing inside eggcases

Left: a newly hatched Small-spotted Catshark

embryo will grow until the yolk has been used up and the young fish completely fills the pouch. At this point it will emerge through the end of the eggcase and swim free, a perfect miniature of its parents, and be left to fend for itself in the open sea.

Over time the abandoned eggcase may work its way free from its anchorage, and being empty and therefore light, will float to the surface where it can be driven ashore by the wind. When beached it may be tangled in drift seaweed on the strandline or blown by strong winds to the back of the beach to be trapped in vegetation. As it dries out it becomes crisp and shrivelled but the tough, leathery material does not rot away like the other organic matter on the beach and can persist for years.

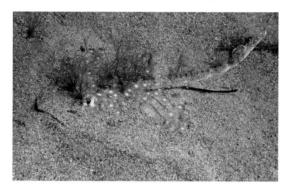

Juvenile Undulate Ray

Elasmobranchs are a vulnerable group of fish because they are relatively slow to reach breeding age, at around 5–10 years, and produce few young when compared to bony fish, only 40 to 150 each year. This has made them particularly susceptible to over-fishing and led to some once common species becoming critically endangered. Recording where their eggcases wash ashore can help to locate their spawning grounds and aid conservation efforts to win much-needed protection for these sites.

A WONDER MATERIAL

Mermaid's purses are made from a material that has intrigued scientists for many years, in particular its resilience against decomposition by the sea and air, attack by bacteria, grazers and predators; and fouling by other marine organisms. Such a material could have a multitude of uses in the biomedical and marine fields. The egg casing, made of a unique blend of collagen proteins, is built up into a multi-layered and cross-linked structure providing both the flexibility and durability to keep the precious embryo safe for a year or more on the sea floor.

Nursehound eggcase on seabed

EGGCASE IDENTIFICATION

Each egg-laying species of elasmobranch has its own, uniquely shaped egg capsule and it is relatively easy to discover which type of shark, skate or ray hatched from it.

First you need to soak your eggcase in water for a few hours. Once rehydrated it should take on its original form and can then be compared to the eggcase identification guide produced by The Shark Trust, which can be download at www.eggcase.org

Now you can measure the size, compare the shape of the 'horns' and note the surface of the capsule – is it smooth and shiny or does it have a flaky or textured exterior?

You can record your findings on the The Great Eggcase Hunt webpage: www.sharktrust.org/recordyoureggcase. This a great way to help with shark conservation by broadening the knowledge of possible shark and ray nursery grounds.

A dried eggcase (left), and the same kind after being rehydrated (right)

Shark eggcases

Two types of shark eggcases are commonly found on British beaches. They are easily distinguished from skate and ray eggcases by their elongated shape and the curly tendrils extending from each corner, which are used to anchor them to seaweed and other seabed structures.

Small-spotted Catshark *Scyliorhinus canicula*

Approximate capsule length 4cm

This shark produces one of the smallest mermaid's purses. These eggcases are sometimes found in clusters with their distinctive curly tendrils tightly entangled, and may even still have their seabed anchor attached. They are usually golden in colour but may be darker or even black, and the capsule feels like smooth plastic.

Nursehound *Scyliorhinus stellaris*

Below: the larger Nursehound eggcase compared to the smaller Small-spotted Catshark eggcase

Approximate capsule length 10cm

This shark produces a larger, more robust version of the Small-spotted Catshark eggcase, with thickened edges.

Skate and ray eggcases

Skate and ray eggcases are squarish in shape and have a pointed horn at each corner. Some have flattened sides called 'keels', while others do not. They tend to be dark brown to black in colour.

Cuckoo Ray *Leucoraja naevus*

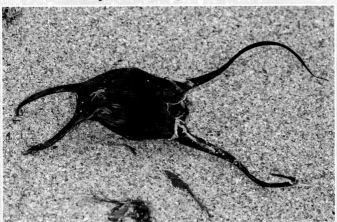

Approximate capsule length 6cm

One of the smallest ray eggcases with a rounded capsule. The top pair of horns are long and curved while the bottom pair are short.

Starry Skate *Amblyraja radiata*

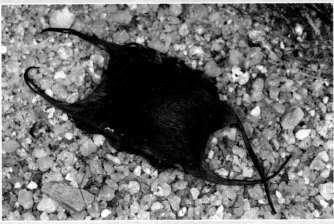

Approximate capsule length 4.5cm

A small, square eggcase with a rough-textured capsule and evenly sized horns.

SKATES AND RAYS

The two groups of elasmobranchs called skates and rays can be difficult to distinguish and there has been some confusion in the past with their English names. In scientific terms, skates lay eggs while rays give birth to live young. For example, the Stingray does not lay eggs while the Starry Skate and White Skate do. However, the smaller British skates have commonly been misnamed as rays, for example the Spotted, Thornback, Small-eyed, Undulate and Blonde Rays, even though they are egg-layers.

Spotted Ray *Raja montagui*

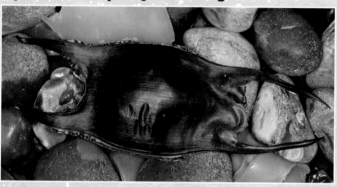

Approximate capsule length 6cm
A small, neat, smooth and usually shiny eggcase. It can be confused with the Undulate Ray (opposite) eggcase, which has a similar appearance but tends to be larger.

Thornback Ray *Raja clavata*

Approximate capsule length 7cm
A medium-sized square eggcase with four short horns, obvious keels along the sides and a dull surface.

Small-eyed Ray *Raja microocellata*

Approximate capsule length 8cm
A medium-sized eggcase which tapers towards the bottom. The top pair of horns are long and wispy while the bottom pair are short. The colour tends towards brown rather than black.

Undulate Ray *Raja undulata*

Approximate capsule length 8cm
A medium-sized eggcase with a similar shape to the Spotted Ray (opposite) but larger. Although it has no keels there is sometimes a tuft of fibre on each side which helps anchor it in place.

Blonde Ray *Raja brachyura*

Approximate capsule length 12cm

A large eggcase with a constriction at one end. It has long horns at the top and short ones at the bottom, obvious keels and sometimes a mat of fibrous material still attached, which would have helped anchor it on the seabed.

White Skate *Rostroraja alba*

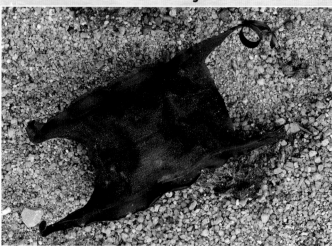

Approximate capsule length 13cm

A very large, robust eggcase with a pair of long, flattened horns at the top which curl at the tips. The keels at the side are very well defined and the surface has a matt finish. So far there are no confirmed records for this eggcase from beaches on mainland UK.

Flapper Skate *Dipturus* cf. *intermedia*

Approximate capsule length 18cm

The Flapper Skate, previously called the Common Skate, is one of the largest skates found around the UK, reaching a size of almost 3m and living for up to 100 years. Its eggcase is also large in relation to those of other species. The eggcases are extremely rare finds around the UK, apart from in a few localities where populations still exist.

Blue Skate *Dipturus* cf. *flossada*

Approximate capsule length 14cm

The Blue Skate has only recently been recognised as a separate species and, along with the Flapper Skate, was previously known as Common Skate. However, the Blue Skate adult and eggcase are slightly smaller than those of Flapper Skate. So far there are no confirmed records for this eggcase from beaches on mainland UK.

Eggs

Lumpsucker *Cyclopterus lumpus*

Lumpsuckers lay their eggs in shallow water where they are exposed to strong wave action, and they regularly wash up onto beaches (see page 148). The eggs are laid in clusters and appear like an irregular, rubbery ball when washed up on the strandline. The individual eggs can easily be made out and sometimes the contours of the rock they were attached to leave an indentation in the clump.

Squid *Loliginidae*

Squid eggs look like long, off-white sausages, or fingers, held together in a cluster, each sausage containing dozens of eggs. On close inspection the individual eggs inside each sausage can be seen. Squid aggregate in shoals for breeding, so the sausages in one cluster may belong to different parents. The adult squid only breed once and then die shortly afterwards. The egg clusters are attached to a seabed anchorage such as seaweed, sea fan, rope or another man-made object, or just partly buried in sand. Stormy weather can dislodge them and wash them ashore.

Common Cuttlefish *Sepia officinalis*

Cuttlefish eggs are sometimes known as sea grapes as they resemble a bunch of black grapes in shape and size. Common Cuttlefish come inshore to breed in spring and summer, laying their egg clusters and attaching them to seaweed, seagrass and man-made objects such as rope and shellfish pots. Each egg contains a single embryo and the cuttlefish's black ink, known as sepia, is injected in to give it the black coloration and obscure the developing embryo inside. Those laid in shallow water are vulnerable to wave action and may be washed ashore in storms. Often the cluster is still wrapped around the seaweed stipe or other object of attachment with a black rubbery material that also binds the eggs together. Depending on their stage of development and how long they have been out of water, they may appear plump like grapes or small and shrivelled like raisins.

Whelk Buccinidae

The spongy egg-masses of Common and Red Whelks are a common sight along British standlines and are known as Seawash Balls. In days past, they were collected and used by mariners for washing in a similar way as bath sponges are used today. The Common Whelk, *Buccinum undatum* (see page 74) is found all around the British coast but the Red Whelk, *Neptunea antiqua*, is more common on northern coasts and is rare in the south. Whelks collect *en masse* for spawning, laying their eggs in small, lens-shaped pouches which are glued together with those of other individuals into a spherical mass. Large egg-masses may contain thousands of egg pouches. Each individual pouch contains around 1,000 eggs, most of which are used to feed the first few individuals that hatch. Once the eggs have hatched the empty egg-mass floats and washes ashore, looking like a grey or off-white irregular ball. However, stormy weather may dislodge unhatched egg-masses which wash ashore looking distinctly yellow in colour. In these the unhatched eggs may be seen inside.

Necklace Shell *Euspira catena*

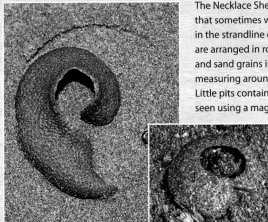

The Necklace Shell (see page 72) lays egg-masses that sometimes wash ashore and can be found in the strandline on sandy beaches. The eggs are arranged in rows, bound together by mucus and sand grains into a collar-shaped open ring measuring around 7cm in diameter and 4cm high. Little pits containing the individual eggs can be seen using a magnifier. The 'collars' are fairly tough and flexible when wet but start to crumble when dry.

The Alder's Necklace Shell, *Euspira pulchella*, lays similar egg-masses but they are much smaller and form a complete ring (inset).

Invertebrates
and their remains

A wide variety of invertebrates and their remains can be found mixed in with seaweeds along the strandline. What is present will depend on where you are in the country and what time of year it is, but listed here are those most commonly found.

Pink Sea Fan *Eunicella verrucosa*

A Pink Sea Fan with the white remains of dead polyps covering the skeleton

Size 30cm

Pink Sea Fans are members of the coral family which form a fan-shaped, branched, tree-like colony made up of many individual polyps that are arranged along the branches. In life, their hard skeleton is covered in soft tissue which is normally pinkish-orange in colour, and occasionally fresh specimens are washed ashore in storms. However, they are most likely to be found on the strandline as brown, twig-like specimens (see opposite) sometimes entangled in fishing line. They can be distinguished from woody twigs by their flexibility, smooth surface and slightly splayed holdfast, and the fact that the branches are normally arranged in one plane rather than in a bushy formation.

As Pink Sea Fans provide a fixed and fairly robust attachment point on the seabed, they are sometimes used by catsharks to attach their eggs and may wash ashore still with the empty eggcases entangled around them.

Right: live Pink Sea Fan polyps

Left: a Pink Sea Fan skeleton stripped of its polyp covering

Dead Man's Fingers *Alcyonium digitatum*

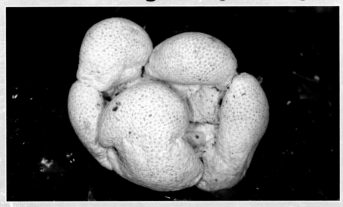

Size 20cm

Dead Man's Fingers is a species of soft coral that grows as a white or orange fleshy lump, forming bloated, finger-like projections covered in tiny polps. They are normally firmly attached to rocks or hard surfaces in areas of fairly strong current but in extremely stormy conditions can sometimes be ripped up by the waves and deposited on the strandline. Here they look like hard, shrivelled, bulbous lumps, covered in tiny dots showing where the individual polyps were.

Hornwrack *Flustra foliacea*

Size 20cm

Commonly found on beach strandlines and often mistaken for a pale seaweed, Hornwrack is actually a colonial animal from the bryozoan or 'sea moss' group. Close inspection with a magnifier of these creamy-grey fronds will reveal the distinctive bryozoan lacy pattern formed by a multitude of tiny 'boxes', which in life would each contain an individual animal called a zooid. This animal has a growing season and sometimes annual growth lines can be seen on the frond. Very fresh specimens have a lemony smell which is lost when dried.

Square-end Hornwrack *Securiflustra securifrons*

Size 10cm

A similar bryozoan to Hornwrack but with more dainty, square-ended fronds. It is usually found in small, ball-like clusters.

Sea Chervil *Alcyonidium diaphanum*

Size variable 10–15cm

Sea Chervil when found on the strandline appears as a brown or golden-brown, spongy or leathery lump which can be variable in shape. It is often lobed or with finger-like projections but can be smooth or knobbly. Take care when handling this item as it can cause an allergic skin reaction, called 'Dogger Bank Itch' suffered by some North Sea fishermen.

Sea Mat *Membranipora membranacea*

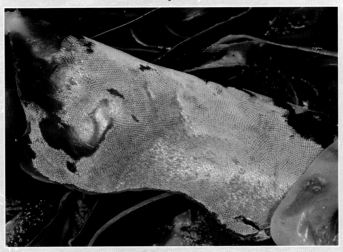

Size 10cm

Sea Mat is an encrusting bryozoan or sea moss, a colonial animal that grows attached to seaweeds. It can be found coating kelp fronds washed up on the strandline, and looks like an off-white lacy material. Observation with a magnifier will clearly reveal the distinctive regular, mesh-like pattern that identifies it as a bryozoan.

Hairy Sea Mat *Electra pilosa*

Size 5cm

This bryozoan often forms discrete patches on seaweeds but is different from *Membranipora membranacea* because of its sharply pointed edges, reminiscent of frost forming on a window. It sometimes forms a tube around narrow red seaweed fronds, such as Irish Moss, and may have a hairy appearance.

HYDROIDS

Hydroids are colonial animals belonging to a larger group called the Cnidaria, which contains animals that catch their prey with the use of stinging cells. The group includes jellyfish and sea anemones. Although superficially a hydroid looks like a plant, examination with a magnifier will reveal the zip-like structure of the fine stems arranged in bushy clusters with rows of angular teeth or cups along them, each home to an individual polyp. Hydroids are not colourful like seaweeds and may lose some of their more delicate features on stranding, making them difficult to identify to species.

On wide sandy beaches with an extended intertidal zone, hydroids and bryozoans can sometimes be the dominant material making up the strandline. The gentle wave action can cause the loose hydroids to roll together, forming an elongated tangle with different species bound together with shells and other debris.

A hydroid roll

Amphisbetia operculata

Size 10cm
This hydroid is usually found on the strandline still attached to the stipe of Cuvie (see page 32) on which it grows, and looks like a thick clump of pale brown hair.

Sea Beard *Nemertesia antennina*

Above: stalked barnacle, *Scalpellum scalpellum*

Size 25cm

Occasionally, after very rough seas, clumps of Sea Beard are thrown up onto the strandline by the waves. Individual colonies are stiff, straight and unbranched but appear covered in fine hairs, resembling a pipe-cleaner, and grow together in clumps held together at the base by a tangled mat of fine rootlets. The creamy-yellow clumps are sometimes colonised at the base by a stalked barnacle called *Scalpellum scalpellum* (inset).

Helter Skelter Hydroid *Hydrallmania falcata*

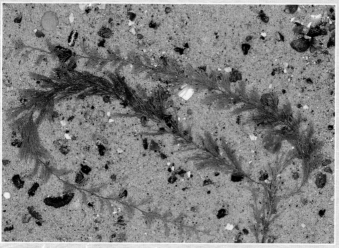

Size 50cm

A long, wispy hydroid with a slender main stem and feather-like branches arranged in a spiral around it. It attaches to shells, pebbles and rocks on sandy or gravelly seabeds.

Sea Fir *Abietinaria abietina*

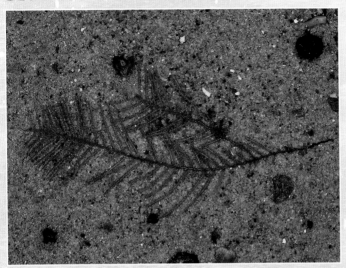

Size 10cm

This brittle hydroid resembles a feather, having a main stem with side branches alternately staggered along it. It grows on shells and rock.

Herringbone Hydroid *Halecium halecinum*

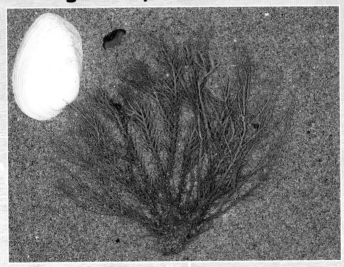

Size 10cm

This colony has a thick main stem with thinner side branches that are parallel and angled, although they may differ in length, to give an overall resemblance to a herring bone. The stiff colonies can grow in clusters, with a holdfast for attachment to rock.

Mermaid's Glove *Haliclona oculata*

Size 30cm

This is an erect sponge that forms a tall, branched structure, sometimes resembling long, thin fingers. Usually pale brown or beige in colour, it has obvious holes along the 'fingers' where the sponge expels water once it has been filtered for nutrients. A similar darker brown sponge, *Raspailia ramosa*, has shorter fingers in a more bushy arrangement and is called the Chocolate Finger Sponge (inset).

Boring Sponge in seashells

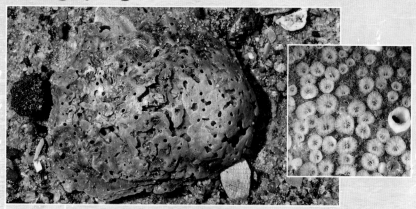

Size Variable

The Boring Sponge, *Cliona celata*, is a sponge that bores into calcium carbonate, typically the shells of marine molluscs such as Common Oyster, Slipper Limpet and Icelandic Cyprine. It secretes a chemical that dissolves the calcium carbonate that the shells are made of and it then inhabits the holes that are formed, protruding from the surface as a small yellow, lobed sponge (inset). Strandline shells of its preferred species often exhibit the holes and patterns left by the sponge.

Sea squirts

Size 2–12cm

Sea squirts (tunicates) are filter-feeding animals that suck in water through one siphon (tube), filter the nutrients from it and eject the waste water through a second siphon. When stranded on the beach they may be attached to seaweed, fishing litter or other debris, or unattached. In appearance they are opaque, with a firm rubbery texture, and may be of a variety of species which are hard to identify from stranded specimens. To confirm your find is a sea squirt, a gentle squeeze should result in a jet of water squirting from the out-siphon (inset), although this should not be done to live specimens in the sea.

Colonial sea squirts are found encrusting litter, kelp stipes and holdfasts. Groups of individual zooids share a single out-siphon. The easiest species to identify is the **Star Sea Squirt**, *Botryllus schlosseri*, with pale, star-shaped groups of individuals on a blue or greenish background.

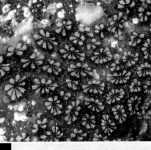

Above: colony of Star Sea Squirts

Left: a live sea squirt with siphons open and lower half encrusted with colonial Star Sea Squirts

Common Starfish *Asterias rubens*

Size 50cm

This starfish can be washed up, sometimes in mass strandings, from shallow water seabeds in rough weather. Starfish belong to the Echinoderm group, which means 'spiny skin'. They have a flexible coat covered in small bumps and usually five arms radiating out in a star shape. Starfish can regenerate lost arms and as a result sometimes specimens are found with fewer arms or with one or more arms of an irregular size. Other starfish species can be found and may have a different number of arms. **Note**: it can be difficult to tell if a starfish is alive or dead so it is worth returning any found to the sea.

Other starfish

Although the Common Starfish is frequently stranded, other types of starfish can sometimes be found washed up. These include the Bloody Henry, Sand Star, Spiny Starfish, and Common Sunstar.

Live Bloody Henry, *Henricia oculata*

Live Sand Star, *Astropecten irregularis*

Stranded Spiny Starfish, *Marthasterias glacialis*

Live Common Sunstar, *Crossaster papposus*

Brittlestars Ophiuroidea

Size Central disc diameter up to 2cm

This group of animals is related to starfish but they have five long, flexible arms radiating from a small central disc. The arms are covered in small spines and are easily broken if handled, hence the English name. Being delicate they are most often found on sandy shore strandlines with one or more arms broken off.

Live brittlestar

Sea Potato *Echinocardium cordatum*

Below: live
Sea Potato
burrowing

Size 5cm

This animal, also called a Heart Urchin, lives buried beneath sandy seabeds and may be washed out by strong waves. The shell or 'test' which encases the animal is very fragile and easily broken but complete specimens are often found, some even with the fine spines still attached, giving them a furry appearance.

FOSSIL SEA POTATOES

Fossilised Sea Potatoes can sometimes be found on beaches and exhibit the same shape and features as modern day Sea Potatoes. They can be found in chalk or flint pebbles of between 65 and 200 million years old, showing that this group of animals have changed little since that time.

Fossilised Sea Potato (left) and fresh Sea Potato test (right)

Edible Sea Urchin *Echinus esculentus*

Below: Mouth parts of a live Edible Sea Urchin

Size 12cm

This large, rounded sea urchin lives on rocky coasts, grazing on algae. The thin, pink test is often broken when found on the strandline, usually without the spines that cover it during life. The mouth parts, known as Aristotle's Lantern, can sometimes be found still attached inside the test but are fragile and easily broken.

ARISTOTLE'S LANTERN

This internal structure, unique to the sea urchin family, resembles the mechanical grabs found in amusement arcades. It consists of five pointed teeth arranged in a circle, the tips of which meet and protrude from the mouth of the animal. It is used to scrape or tear algae which it then chews by moving the teeth from side to side. The ancient Greek philospher, Aristotle, first named this structure after a type of lantern that was common in his day. These five-sided lanterns were made of horn which sheltered the flame inside whilst allowing the light to shine through. The name has stuck for thousands of years.

Green Sea Urchin *Psammechinus miliaris*

Size 5cm

A slightly flattened sea urchin of rocky shores (and other marine habitats), covered in green spines tipped with purple. It covers itself with pebbles, shells, pieces of seaweed and other debris. The green tests can be found on the strandline and are often complete.

A live Green Sea Urchin

Sea Mouse *Aphrodita aculeata*

Above: a live Sea Mouse

The underside looks tough and leathery

Size 20cm

This is a species of scale worm which lives buried beneath sandy seabeds, and may occasionally be washed out by strong waves. It has a covering of long, iridescent bristles and both these and its size give it the appearance of a bedraggled mouse.

Sand Mason tubes *Lanice conchilega*

Size 20cm

Sand Mason worms construct a distinctive branched tube made of mucus and course sand grains in which they live. On sandy seashores there may be dense aggregations of these, looking like miniature trees at low tide. Strong waves can dislodge the tubes and sometimes large numbers of them wash onto the strandline.

Parchment Worm tubes *Chaetopterus variopedatus*

Size 20cm
This worm constructs a U-shaped tube in which it lives buried in sand. The buff-coloured tubes, when found on the strandline, appear shrivelled and papery.

Pectinaria belgica tube

Size 9cm
This straight-sided, tapering tube is constructed of sand grains. The empty tubes are normally found on sandy beaches. In life, the worm lives head down beneath the sand in the wider end of the tube, with the narrow end protruding above the surface.

Keelworm tubes *Spirobranchus* spp.

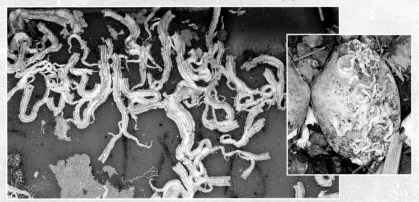

Size 2.5cm

Keelworms construct white, calcareous tubes which can be found on the strandline attached to seashells or fishing litter that has been on the seabed for some time. The wider end of the long tube is open while the tapered end is sealed. Those attached to long-haul litter may not be of local origin, making identification to species level difficult.

Acorn barnacles

Above: live acorn barnacle with feeding tentacles extended

Size Up to 3cm

A variety of acorn barnacle species can be found attached to seashells or litter found on the strandline. They are commonly recorded on fishing litter, especially crab pots that have spent some time on the seabed, but also on long-haul drifting items where they may have attached as larvae in the surface waters. Identification of this crustacean to species level can be difficult and requires noting the shape of the opening and number of plates making up the shell. Some species occur on both sides of the Atlantic.

113

Tangle balls

Size Variable

Spherical masses of tangled animal and plant matter, sometimes mixed in with man-made litter. They are formed by debris on the sea floor which is rolled together by wave action into a ball and thrown up on the strandline where they retain their shape. Depending on where around the coast they are they may contain plant roots, seaweed, hydroids, fishing line and plastic objects.

Sea foam

Sea foam, also known as spume, forms when dissolved organic material in seawater is churned up by strong winds and breaking waves close to shore. This material includes proteins and fats from decaying marine algae and plankton and its creation is a natural process. The breaking waves mix air in with the organic particles, resulting in foam washing onto beaches with the waves. Occasionally, as a result of large plankton blooms offshore, several metres of foam can build up on the beach. On rare occasions this can swamp coastal roads.

Cuttlefish and squid

Cuttlefish and squid are molluscs, members of the cephalopod group which also includes octopus. Cuttlefish have an internal gas-filled shell or 'bone' which is used to control buoyancy. By increasing or decreasing the amount of gas in the bone they can rise or sink in the water column. They are ambush predators, using their ability to instantly change their skin colour and texture for camouflage and thus surprise unwary prey. Cuttlefish breed only once and having produced their eggs they die leaving just

A juvenile cuttlefish, a miniature version of the adult.

the bone to float on the sea and wash up on beaches. Cuttlebone is a very common strandline item, found all around the coast.

Cuttlebones are made of calcium carbonate and have been used by man for several purposes, including as a dietary supplement for pet birds and reptiles, in powder form as an addition to toothpaste, and carved to make moulds for casting silver jewellery and small objects.

Squid and their bones are less frequently stranded, although they are sometimes found as discarded angling bait.

Complete cuttlefish sometimes wash up before the soft tissue has decomposed to reveal the cuttlebone.

CUTTLEFISH INK

The scientific name for cuttlefish, *Sepia*, is a clue to another historic use for cuttlefish. Both the ancient Greeks and Romans extracted the reddish-brown pigment called sepia from the ink sacs of cuttlefish for writing and drawing, and named the animal after it. Cuttlefish release the ink using it as a 'smoke-screen' to hide their escape from predators.

Although most cuttlebones found are from the Common Cuttlefish, those from two other species occasionally wash up on British shores.

Common Cuttlefish *Sepia officinalis*

Size 40cm
The largest and most widespread cuttlefish, commonly found all around Britain. The bone has almost parallel sides.

Elegant Cuttlefish *Sepia elegans*

Size 9cm
The smallest-boned cuttlefish, this species lives in offshore waters off western Britain. The bone is rarely found and is sharply tapered with a central raised keel.

Pink Cuttlefish *Sepia orbignyana*

Size 14cm
A medium-sized cuttlefish rarely seen off SW Britain. The bone is narrowly oval in shape but with a long spine which usually remains intact. The bone often has a pink tinge.

Squid Loliginidae

Size 75cm

The shells of squid are reduced to a very thin, transparent, internal bone called a 'pen'. They look and feel like a plastic version of a feather or quill.

Ram's Horn Squid *Spirula spirula*

Size 4.5cm

Despite the name this animal is not technically a squid but is the only known species from its group, the Spirulida. However, it is related to both squid and cuttlefish, all of which are cephalopods. The Ram's Horn Squid lives in the open ocean and is unusual in having an internal, coiled, chambered shell which is used for buoyancy in a similar way to cuttlebones. The distinctive shells are not a common feature of strandlines in the UK, but they are more commonly found in southern Europe.

Crab moults

Wandering along the strandline it can be alarming to find what looks like an abundance of dead crabs. It is more likely that these are just their empty moulted shells. Check by picking one up – if it feels light and doesn't smell bad, try putting a finger nail under the back of the carapace to see if you can flip it open. The inside of a moulted shell looks empty except for the remains of the gills.

Crabs have a hard external covering for protection and for the attachment of their muscles – their exoskeleton. As they grow this 'shell' does not grow or stretch and gets increasingly tight. Eventually the crab will start to produce a chemical to separate the exoskeleton from the tissue inside and to dissolve a seam at the back of the carapace. At the same time it will take in water to swell its body until the softened seam bursts, allowing the animal to carefully climb out of its small shell. Immediately the size difference between the swelled crab and its old shell can be seen and the empty moult is abandoned, complete with leg and eye coverings and looking just like a dead crab. Being light these moults float in water and wash up onto the strandline. Meanwhile the soft crab will hide away for a few days while its outer surface hardens into a new and bigger shell.

Collecting and comparing moulted shells is a good way to identify different types of crab and discover which species live adjacent to a particular beach. As crab moults are relatively fragile the carapace is the part most often found, although whole moults are common, especially during the summer when crab populations are swelled by growing juveniles. Below are some of the commoner crab moults found on beaches. Crab shells often lose their original colour after some time in the strandline but shape and other characteristics enable identification.

Shore Crab *Carcinus maenas*

Size 8cm
The most widespread species of crab, found in all intertidal habitats. A roughly heart-shaped carapace with five teeth at either side of the eyes and three rounded lobes between the eyes. All walking legs are pointed and not flattened. If fresh it should be greenish or brown in colour.

Velvet Swimming Crab *Necora puber*

Below: live Velvet Swimming Crab

Size 8cm

A very common crab with a roughly heart-shaped carapace which is covered in fine hairs, giving it a velvety texture. Blue markings on the shell, claws and legs are distinctive. The back pair of legs are flattened into paddles for swimming. The edge of the carapace is sharply serrated and there are spikes on the claws. In life, the red eyes and aggressive nature of this crab have inspired the alternative name of Devil Crab.

Edible Crab *Cancer pagurus*

Above: claw moult from an Edible Crab

Size Up to 25cm

A common crab with an orange-brown, oval-shaped shell with a distinctive 'pie-crust' edge. The large claws have black tips and all the walking legs are pointed. This is the very familiar, commercially fished species, and offshore individuals grow much larger than those found inshore.

Common Spider Crab *Maja squinado*

Above: Common Spider Crab tail flap

Size 20cm

A large crab with a teardrop-shaped shell covered in spines and tubercles, with a sharply serrated edge to the carapace and a pair of horn-like spines between the eyes. When fresh it is orange in colour and has long, thin, pointed legs and claws which often become detached so that carapace, legs and claws are found separately. One of the commonest parts of the moult found on strandlines is the segmented, triangular tail flap.

Four-horned Spider Crab *Pisa tetraodon*

Size 4cm

A master of camouflage, this small spider crab lives amongst seaweed where it is almost invisible thanks to the covering of algae it plants on its shell. The strandline moults can remain covered in algae.

CRYPTIC CRABS

Spider crabs are a varied group, using their thin, tweezer-like claws to snip seaweed, sponges and other marine life, using them to decorate their shells for camouflage. The spines on their shells, legs and claws provide a rough surface for attachment, creating a collage of colour and texture. This decoration enables them to blend in perfectly with their surroundings, often rendering them invisible until they move. If they relocate they redecorate, hence their alternative name of decorator crabs.

Above: This Long-legged Spider Crab, *Macropodia rostrata*, was spotted whilst diving. As we watched it walking along, a clump of seaweed drifted by and the crab stepped into it and simply vanished. On close inspection we found that the seaweed already contained two other crabs of the same species. If we had not seen it happen, the crabs would have been completely invisible to us.

Left: You would have to look very hard to spot this live Four-horned Spider Crab

Masked Crab *Corystes cassivelaunus*

Male Masked Crab with long claws

Size 4cm

A crab of sandy shores where it burrows beneath the surface. The carapace is pale pink in colour and roughly oval. Its distinctive feature is the long, bristly antennae which are locked together to form a breathing tube to the surface when the crab is buried. The carapace has ridges in the shape of a face, hence the English name. Males have elongated claws.

Female Masked Crab with short claws

Pennant's Swimming Crab *Portumnus latipes*

Size 2cm

This small crab has beautiful white markings on a sandy, shield-shaped carapace. The fragile moults can be found in large numbers on sandy beaches, where the crab burrows just beneath the surface. The back pair of legs are flattened.

Angular Crab *Goneplax rhomboides*

Below: Live Angular Crab

Size 4cm

This crab has a rectangular carapace with very long claws. The pale, sandy-coloured carapace has a sharp spine at each front corner and the eyes are on long stalks which can fold back into it. It lives in branching burrows in sandy mud seabeds.

123

Henslow's Swimming Crab *Polybius henslowii*

Size 4.5cm

This is a rarely found crab on British strandlines and is unusual in that it spends most of its life in the surface waters, often in swarms, where it feeds on sardines and squid. It has a thin, rounded shell and all four pairs of walking legs are flattened and fringed with hairs to aid swimming.

Hermit crabs Paguridae

Below: A live hermit crab using a whelk shell for protection

Size Up to 3.5cm

Hermit crabs are a separate group from true crabs as their elongated abdomen is not protected by a shell, and instead they inhabit discarded mollusc shells. The crabs' own reduced shell covers their claws and front two pairs of legs, one claw being much larger than the other. The moults of these can sometimes be found on the strandline, mostly on sandy shores. There are several species that may be found.

Other crustacean moults

Shrimp and prawn moults

Size Up to 11cm

Occasionally the delicate, transparent moults of a variety of shrimps and prawns can be found washed up on sandy beaches. They are difficult to identify to species level but are characterised by elongated bodies covered in a series of shell plates ending with a tailfan.

Lobster *Homarus gammarus*

Size Up to 100cm

Moults of the familiar Lobster are not often found on the strandline as the animal tends to eat its moulted shell as a source of calcium, to help it grow a new one. However, occasionally parts of it can be found, in particular the large, tough claws. In life, Lobsters are blue, a distinguishing feature of moults. Sometimes orange moults can be found but these are probably the remains of someone's beach barbecue.

Carcasses, skulls and bones

Seabirds and their remains

Dead seabirds are common finds on beaches, especially in the winter when rough seas might make food harder to find. They can also be victims of pollution incidents at sea or entanglement in debris. Of course a wide variety of birds might end up dead on the strandline, from racing pigeons to pheasants, crows to birds of prey. However, this section concentrates on seabirds and shorebirds.

Seabirds can be found in a variety of conditions from live but injured or oiled birds to dead complete specimens, or just skulls and other bones. If you find a bird on the beach that clearly needs rescuing, we advise calling the RSPCA or local animal

Herring Gull having swallowed a fishing line

Storm-wrecked Atlantic Puffin

rescue centre as quickly as possible, giving them a precise location and accurate description of the birds' condition.

Complete, dead birds might be ringed so it is worth checking the legs for this. Bird ringing provides a lot of information about how far seabirds travel and how long they live. Auks for example, can live for more than 40 years. If it is possible to either retrieve the ring or note what is written on it, the organisation involved would be grateful for the information.

Even if just the skull remains, the species can be identified from its size and shape. The bill, when fresh, is covered in a thin, coloured sheath which is often lost, leaving just the bone. The sheath might help with identification but the shape of the bill is also key.

Bird rings

Left: dead juvenile Loggerhead Turtle

Auks

The auks are a group of seabirds that spend their winter offshore feeding and rafting at sea. They only come ashore to breed, often in large, mixed colonies. They are the northern hemisphere's equivalent to penguins, some species diving to depths of over 100m, and like penguins, they beat their wings underwater to propel themselves, chasing prey such as squid, sandeels and other fish.

Atlantic Puffin

Guillemot *Uria aalge*

Size 10cm
The most common auk skull found on beaches is that of the Guillemot with its sharp, dagger-like bill. The sheath is black.

Razorbill *Alca torda*

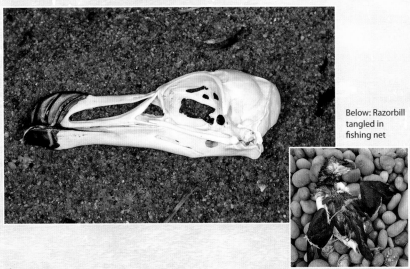

Below: Razorbill tangled in fishing net

Size 8cm

Less numerous than the Guillemot and therefore less commonly found except following pollution incidents and seabird-wrecks (see page 134), the Razorbill has a deep, hooked bill with the sharp tip on the top overlapping the bottom. The sheath is black, sometimes still with its white stripe.

Atlantic Puffin *Fratercula arctica*

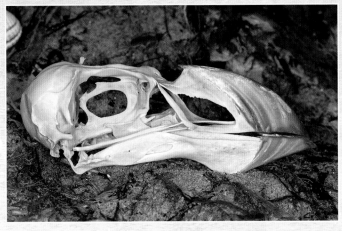

Size 8cm

Not such a common find as the other auks but may be found in numbers following a pollution incident or seabird-wreck (see page 134). During the breeding season, the Puffin's bill is covered in a colourful sheath which is shed in winter and replaced by a duller one. The bill is triangular in shape.

129

Gulls

There are several gull species around the UK, any of which could be found on the strandline. They vary in their feeding habits with correspondingly varied bill shapes and sizes. To add to the confusion, gulls' bill-sheaths can vary with age and season. Here we illustrate a few examples showing the contrast between a small and medium-sized species and the world's largest.

Black-headed Gull *Chroicocephalus ridibundus*

Size 7cm

A small and relatively common gull, regularly found on the strandline. The skull is small with delicate bones. The bill is pointed and slightly hooked.

Herring Gull *Larus argentatus*

Size 9cm

A medium-sized gull, a familiar bird frequenting fishing villages and seaside resorts.

Great Black-backed Gull *Larus marinus*

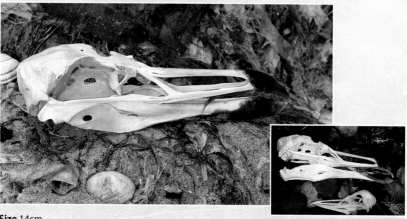

Size 14cm

A large gull and a fierce predator of other seabirds, small mammals and fish, this bird has a large skull and robust, hooked bill.

Above: comparative sizes of the Great Black-backed (above) and Black-headed (below) Gulls

Other seabirds

Gannet *Morus bassanus*

Above: dead Gannet entangled in marine litter

Size 18cm

The largest of our European seabirds, the Gannet has a correspondingly large skull with a robust, very smooth, straight and sharply pointed bill. Gannets are plunge-divers, spotting fish from the air and diving from great heights to catch them, folding back their wings to make themselves stream-lined for hitting the water. The skull is specially adapted to cope with hitting the water at high speed, with built-in shock-absorbing air sacs and nostrils that open inside the bill to prevent water gushing in. The sheath is a creamy-grey colour.

Oystercatcher *Haematopus ostralegus*

Size 11cm

Oystercatchers are common birds of seashores, with distinctive black-and-white plumage and long orange bills. The skull is small with a long, straight, robust bill, with an orange-tinted sheath.

Fulmar *Fulmarus glacialis*

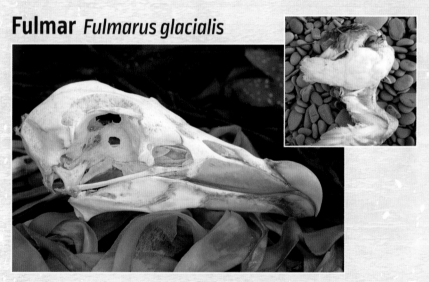

Size 9cm

The Fulmar belongs to a group of birds called 'tube-noses' which also contains albatrosses, petrels and shearwaters. Tube-nose refers to their specially adapted nostrils which are raised above the bill. Although the tube-shaped nostril sheaths may be lost during decomposition, the elongated holes of the nostrils can be seen on the upper surface of the bill. The tip of the bill is sharply hooked and the sheath is browny-yellow.

Shearwater Procellariidae

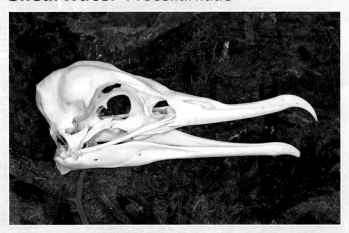

A number of different species of shearwater visit the UK. They are members of the tubenose family along with the more commonly found Fulmar. They are true seabirds only coming ashore for breeding. The skull has the typical elongated nostrils and hook-tipped bill of this group. Skulls are difficult to identify to species level unless the fresh specimen of a complete bird is found.

Sternum

Often mistaken for the skull of some mysterious creature, bird sternums or breast-bones are commonly found on strandlines. The flat bone and central ridge or keel is for the attachment of powerful flight muscles that make up the bird's breast.

STORM-WRECKED SEABIRDS

In the winter of 2013–2014, a series of severe storms battered north-west Europe. In January and February 2014, unnaturally high numbers of dead seabirds appeared on south and west coast beaches of the UK, and in the Bay of Biscay. A conservative estimate recorded in excess of 30,000 birds, although thousands more would have been lost at sea or washed ashore and not recorded.

Of the 27 species identified in this storm-wreck, the majority were auks. Puffins bore the brunt of the disaster with more than 15,000 recorded, followed by Guillemots and Razorbills. The birds were in very poor condition, severely underweight and with little or no food in their stomachs. Some were also entangled or oiled. The data from ringed birds showed which breeding colonies they were from, enabling future monitoring and assessment of the impact.

Seabirds are under increasing pressure from litter, pollution and overfishing of their prey species. Well-fed, healthy seabirds are equipped to cope with Atlantic winter storms but the declining health and resilience of populations results in poorly equipped birds. Whilst the severity of the 2013/14 winter storms had a devastating impact on already weak seabird populations, this storm-wreck also gave us an insight into the plight of these birds out on the open sea where it is normally hidden from view.

This incident is unlikely to be the only one of its kind and other causes such as pollution spills can also result in large numbers of seabirds washing ashore. Beachcombers are often the first to notice unusual events such as these and should report anything of concern that they find.

Live strandings of cetaceans and turtles

In the event of finding a live cetacean or turtle stranding it is vital to report it immediately to either the police, RSPCA or BDMLR (British Divers Marine Life Rescue), who are equipped and trained to rescue these species. It is important to report the exact location and as much detail as possible to aid the rescue. A phone-camera photo may help. We advise that untrained individuals do not attempt to approach the animal but keep other people and pets away. It is NOT advisable to attempt refloating stranded animals and may cause them more harm.

Injured Grey Seal pup

Seals are more likely to be found on beaches where they regularly haul out at low tide and during the pupping season. At this time pups may be found alone but this is not necessarily cause for concern and the mother may be just offshore waiting to return. If there are obvious signs of injury or malnutrition the above authorities should be notified. Otherwise we suggest monitoring the pup from a distance to see if the mother returns and if you are still concerned about its condition contact the rescue agencies.

Contacts
BDMLR hotline: 01825 765546 (office hours) or 07787 433412 (out of hours)
RSPCA hotline (England & Wales): 0300 1234 999
SSPCA hotline (Scotland): 03000 999 999

Dead strandings of cetaceans and turtles

Dead mammals can end up on beaches for a number of reasons. Marine animals may die at sea from natural causes or as a result of human impact, and can, under certain circumstances, wash ashore. On land, wild or farm animals may fall from cliffs or be washed down rivers into the sea.

The first sign of a carcass on the beach might be the smell, although the actual remains may not be immediately obvious. While these finds can offer an interesting insight into animals we wouldn't otherwise get to see close up, they need to be approached with caution as mammals can carry transferable diseases, and both people and pets should avoid direct contact.

Whales, dolphins and porpoises belong to the same taxonomic order and are collectively called cetaceans. Cetaceans can be divided into two main groups – those with teeth and those with baleen. Baleen whales include the Blue, Fin and Humpback Whales which use fibrous baleen plates to sieve small animals such as fish and krill from the water (see page 146). Toothed cetaceans include porpoises, dolphins, pilot whales and the world's largest predator, the Sperm Whale, all of which have stranded on British shores.

A variety of marine mammals may be found around the British coast and they can be hard to identify to species level, depending on state of decomposition and damage. For that reason this book does not aim to describe animals to species level.

On occasion, a scarce species of cetacean is found offering an extremely rare opportunity to study an animal that we know virtually nothing about. In addition, vital information on the threats cetaceans, seals and turtles face is being gathered from dead strandings found around our coastline. It is therefore important to photograph and report to the UK Cetacean Strandings Investigation Programme (CSIP) any you find, to increase our knowledge about these elusive animals.

Contacts
CSIP hotline: 0800 6520333
CSIP: www.ukstrandings.org

Sheep skeleton

136

INVESTIGATING STRANDINGS

Cetacean strandings have been recorded in the UK for more than 100 years, initially by the Natural History Museum and more recently through a collaborative project, the Cetacean Strandings Investigation Programme (CSIP) which is funded by the UK government. In recent years both turtle and Basking Shark strandings have been added and a proportion of all strandings recorded are recovered for post-mortem examination. This long-term research gives an insight into the diseases, health status and threats to cetaceans, turtles and Basking Sharks in UK waters, and highlights any trends in causes of mortality.

More information about the CSIP and how to report a stranding can be found at www.ukstrandings.org

Recording a dead stranded Common Dolphin for the CSIP

Whales

Dead juvenile Fin Whale, *Balaenoptera physalus*

Size Up to 30m

The majority of animals that die at sea never reach land but rarely, dead whales can be found. Most of the large whales have the characteristic throat pleats that identify them as baleen whales. The only large toothed whale is the Sperm Whale, *Physeter macrocephalus,* which has a distinctive square-shaped head. Smaller-toothed whales such as pilot whales and beaked whales also regularly strand.

Dead Long-fin Pilot Whale, *Globicephala melas*

Dolphins

Left: Stranded Common Dolphin, *Delphinus delphis*

Below: stranded newborn Risso's Dolphin, *Grampus griseus*

Size Up to 4m

Dolphins are normally distinguished from whales by their smaller size. A variety of species strand around our coastline and not all have the familiar dolphin-shaped beak. Size, skin coloration and shape of dorsal fin are normally used to identify a live species but this is usually difficult unless the carcass is very fresh.

SHARK BITE

A dead stranded Common Dolphin, *Delphinus delphis*, found in Dorset in 2014 had an unusual injury which we believed to be caused by a shark bite. An expert agreed and explained that in some dolphins parasites are found in the blubber around the reproductive areas, which is the area of the body most likely to be bitten by a predatory or scavenging shark. It is thought that this parasite has also evolved to spend part of its lifecycle in a shark – an amazing example of parasitic evolution. The story also illustrates how, by sharing our beachcombing finds, we can learn so much more about the natural world around us.

Porpoise

Size Up to 1.7m

There is only one species of porpoise in the UK, the Harbour Porpoise, *Phocoena phocoena*. It is the smallest of all our cetaceans and its small size, blunt head and tiny, spade-shaped teeth identify it.

WHALE LICE

A whale louse is a parasitic crustacean of the family Cyamidae, these lice are found on all types of cetacean. Many species of cetacean have their own species of louse. Lice are commonly found in areas of the host's body that are protected from water flow, such as the mouth, blow hole and around the eyes or in skin lesions. The lice are flattened with

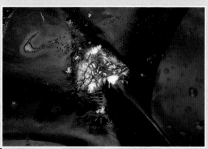

the rear pairs of legs designed to grip, to prevent being washed away. They feed on algae settling on the host's body and on flaking skin, causing only minor skin damage on healthy animals.

Above: Common Dolphin lesion infested with whale lice
Left: close up of a whale louse

Seals

Stranded Common Seal

Size Up to 2.1m

There are two native species of seal in the UK, the Common (Harbour) Seal, *Phoca vitulina*, and the Grey Seal, *Halichoerus grypus*. Their carcasses are easily distinguished from those of cetaceans by their clawed flippers and tail (as opposed to fins and a fluke). Other distinguishing features, if fresh enough, include fur and head shape.

Grey Seals give birth during the autumn and winter months and seasonal storms often separate mothers from young. Pups are born with a distinctive creamy white coat which is lost after 2–4 weeks. At certain times of year dead 'white coats' may be found.

Dead Grey Seal (above) and live white-coat Grey Seal (left)

Seal tags

When seal pups are rescued, rehabilitated and returned to the sea, rescue organisations often attach a plastic tag to the back flippers. Future records of the tag can provide information about how well the seal is doing and how far it travels. Any tags found on dead seals should contain the contact details of the rescue organisation and individual reference number of the seal, to enable the information to be passed on.

Turtles

Dead juvenile
Loggerhead
Turtle

Size Up to 2.4m

The Leatherback Turtle, *Dermochelys coriacea,* is the only species of turtle that frequents our colder British waters, coming here to feed on jellyfish from its breeding grounds in the Caribbean. However, other species of turtle occasionally arrive here after straying off course. Unable to survive the cold sea temperatures they die and may then wash ashore. These include the Loggerhead Turtle, *Caretta caretta,* Hawksbill Turtle, *Eretmochelys imbricata,* Green Turtle, *Chelonia mydas,* and Kemp's Ridley Turtle, *Lepidochelys kempii,* all of which have been recorded in the UK.

Leatherback Turtles are easily distinguished from all other species by their lack of a hard shell and their enormous size, being the largest turtles in the world. They are unusual among reptiles in being able to internally regulate their body temperature, enabling them as adults to migrate to cold-water feeding grounds.

All species of turtle may strand as a result of drowning through entanglement in rope and netting or through ingestion of marine litter such as balloons, plastic bags and other debris (see pages 229–232).

Leatherback
Turtle carapace

Marine mammal skeletal remains

Carcasses stranded on beaches break down quickly, due to a combination of scavenging by invertebrates and birds and decomposition by bacteria. The wind and sun then bleach exposed skeletal remains, leaving clean bones and other items to be found.

Gulls scavenging the carcass of a Fin Whale, *Balaenoptera physalus*

Dolphin vertebrae

Identification of species from bones is not possible in the field but size is an indicator of whether a vertebra belonged to a dolphin or whale. Single or joined vertebrae and even complete spinal columns can occasionally be found, as can the intervertebral discs (inset) which give flexibility to the spine. The long processes at the top (dorsal spine) and the sides (transverse processes) are typical of marine mammals and are for the attachment of powerful muscles used for swimming. However not all their vertebrae have these, for example those at the neck and tail lack them.

Marine mammal skulls

The skulls of different species of cetacean can sometimes be identified to species by looking at the size and shape of the skull and the arrangement of teeth or baleen. For example, the Harbour Porpoise skull is very small with spade-shaped teeth, Risso's Dolphins have a small number of rounded teeth only on the lower jaw, Bottlenose Dolphins are large, robust animals when compared to the much smaller Common Dolphin which has a long beak and many small, pointed teeth.

Top view of skull of Risso's Dolphin, *Grampus griseus*

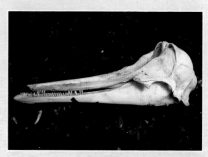

Side view of skull of Common Dolphin, *Delphinus delphis*

Top view of skull of Fin Whale, *Balaenoptera physalus*

Underside of Fin Whale skull

Side view of skull of Harbour Porpoise, *Phocoena phocoena*

Side view of skull of Grey Seal, *Halichoerus grypus*

Marine mammal ear bones

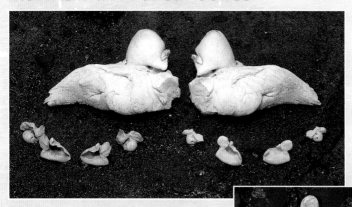

Fin Whale ear bones (top), dolphin ear bones (bottom left) and Harbour Porpoise ear bones (bottom right)

The ear bones of marine mammals look different to other bones and easily become separated from the skull as the carcass decomposes. They vary between species, but are often sculptured and folded with a glossy surface.

Grey Seal ear bone

Whale bones

Fin Whale vertebra

Bones from whale carcasses are much more rarely found but size and robustness is the best indication of origin. A bit of local or internet investigation may reveal information about a certain type of whale stranding on the beach in question, solving the puzzle of what species the bones are from.

Whale baleen

Fin Whale baleen

Baleen whales are so-called because they use baleen plates instead of teeth to catch their food. A row of tightly packed baleen plates hang from either side of the upper jaw and, depending on the species and age of the individual, can measure over 1 metre in length. Plates are made of keratin (like our hair and nails) with a frayed inner edge of fine or coarse hair-like strands. The animal takes large gulps of water filled with small fish or plankton and then uses its tongue to push the water out between the baleen plates. The food gets caught on the hairs, which act like a sieve before being licked off and swallowed.

Baleen has a plastic-like, flexible quality and historically was called 'whale-bone' and used to strengthen ladies' corsets among other uses.

Ambergris

Ambergris is a substance produced in the intestines of a small proportion of Sperm Whales, it is thought as a reaction to the sharp squid beaks (squid being their staple food) passing through their system. Eventually lumps of it are passed and float in the sea, where, over time, they change in consistency, colour and odour. It is notoriously hard to identify as its appearance can vary widely, although generally it is hard with a waxy texture, often rounded and worn by the sea. The best way to identify a piece of ambergris is by its smell, which is said to be earthy and animalistic. When fresh the smell is offensive but after months or years at sea the fragrance becomes more subtle, sweet and appealing. Another clue is the presence of squid beaks inside the lump. Historically, ambergris has been highly prized and used by the perfume industry, although alternative, synthetic substitutes are now available. Even so, some pieces of ambergris, if properly matured, can be worth a great deal of money, although many are not so valuable.

Charlie Naysmith found this lump of ambergris while beachcombing on a Dorset beach

Fish

Many species of fish can be found washed ashore on beaches and there are a number of reasons why they might have ended up there. Animals that inhabit shallow water can be accidentally thrown up by big waves, especially if their place of shelter is disturbed. Some fish do not survive being caught by commercial or sport fishermen, even when released alive, and may be washed ashore. Others might be dropped by seabirds or chased out of the shallows by predators. Occasionally a real rarity might be found, such as a Sunfish or Pufferfish. The skeletal remains of a bony fish may be all that is left of a stranding. Fish bones are distinguished from bird or mammal bones by being very thin, brittle and with an almost translucent quality. Here are some of the most common species you may come across.

Dead Short-snouted Seahorse found on a Dorset beach

Lumpsucker *Cyclopterus lumpus*

Size Up to 55cm

This rotund fish is very distinctive in appearance, with rows of bumps along its length and a large, powerful sucker made of modified pelvic fins on its underside. Lumpsuckers come into shallow water in late winter and early spring to lay their eggs on rocky seabeds. The male fish is left to guard the developing eggs, using his sucker to anchor himself. During low spring tides he can be left exposed in the shallow water where he is vulnerable to crashing waves, exposure to strong sunlight and even seabird attack. However, he will not desert his post, even though it may result in his death (see page 94 for Lumpsucker eggs).

Small-spotted Catshark *Scyliorhinus canicula*

Above: close up
of shark skin

Size Up to 75cm

This is one of the smallest of our native sharks, sometimes called a dogfish. In some areas it is a fairly common find on strandlines, usually as a result of commercial fishery bycatch or discard by sport anglers. It has flat teeth for crushing its prey and these can sometimes be seen in dried-up specimens. The skin is covered in minute tooth-like denticles, designed to reduce turbulence and improve swimming efficiency. This makes it very rough to the touch, which is why historically its skin has been used as sand-paper for smoothing wood and also as a binding on sword hilts, to prevent them slipping from sweaty hands in battle.

Skates and rays Rajidae

Size Up to 125cm

Dead skates and rays are sometimes found on beaches intact or with the wings removed, and it may be difficult to identify them to species level from a carcass. The long, spiny tail and ventral gills and mouth are distinguishing features of rays.

BONELESS

Sharks, skates and rays are unlike bony fish in that their skeleton is made entirely of cartilage, a more flexible material than rigid bone. Occasionally the cartilaginous remains of these animals can be found on the beach and can cause confusion as to what exactly they are. The cartilage can be mistaken for plastic or another man-made substance and the shape is unfamiliar.

Pearlside *Maurolicus muellery*

Size Up to 6.5cm

A deepwater species that occasionally gets cast ashore, this small fish is typically found at depths of around 1,000m where there is virtually no light. It has rows of small light organs called photophores along its underside, probably as a defence from predators below to camouflage it against light coming down from above. At night it moves to surface waters to feed, migrating back to depth during daylight hours.

Grey Triggerfish *Balistes capriscus*

Above: Trigger-fish spine

Size Up to 60cm

Found on strandlines in the colder months, this is a relatively new species to British waters which has become more common over the last few decades. The name derives from a specialised mechanism in the dorsal fin designed to protect it from predators. One fin-ray locks a second in an erect position so that the fish can wedge itself into narrow crevices if threatened. The mechanism then releases the locked spine to enable the fish to come out.

Grey Triggerfish live in oceanic water and are commonly found sheltering beneath drifting objects, including litter. It is possible that these fish travel here with the increasing amounts of rafting debris from the Atlantic Ocean (see page 206).

Ballan Wrasse *Labrus bergylta*

Size Up to 50cm

These are common fish in shallow, coastal waters and are quite variable in colour. There are a number of reasons why they might end up on the strandline, including partial predation by marine mammals or being caught out by stormy weather. They feed on molluscs and crustaceans and in order to deal with the protective shells of their prey they have strong teeth in their jaws and also crushing teeth on a plate in their throat. These pharyngeal teeth and their plate are called a Ballan Cross and historically have been carried by mariners as a good-luck charm to protect them from drowning. The Ballan Cross (inset) often remains after the fish has decomposed.

Boar Fish *Capros aper*

Size Up to 30cm

A distinctive, small orange fish with large eyes. Normally living in relatively deep water, it occasionally moves into shallow coastal water and sometimes washes ashore onto the strandline. Although it is more common further south than the British Isles, in some years it appears in good numbers in the western English Channel and strandline sightings have become more frequent in recent years.

Seahorses *Hippocampus* spp.

Size Up to 16cm

Finding a seahorse on the strandline is a surprisingly frequent occurrence on some coasts as seahorses migrate to shallow water to breed. As they are not strong swimmers they may get washed up with loose seaweed and eelgrass in rough weather. They are also taken by gulls and other seabirds which may then drop them, possibly finding them unpalatable.

There are two British species of seahorse, the Spiny Seahorse, *Hippocampus guttulatus* (right), and the Short-snouted Seahorse, *Hippocampus hippocampus* (left). Occasionally live strandings are found and it is worth returning them to the sea in this instance.

UNDER THREAT

On a global scale, wild seahorse populations are under threat for a number of reasons. By far the worst threat comes from the traditional Chinese medicine trade, which takes more than

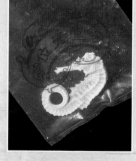

100 million seahorses each year. They are believed to be effective as an aphrodisiac, to promote growth in children and as a substitute for Botox, amongst other things. In addition, around 1 million dead seahorses each year are also sold in shell and gift shops as marine curios.

Live Spiny Seahorse (left) and a seahorse used in Traditional Chinese Medicine (right)

Pipefish Syngnathinae

Left and above:
Greater Pipefish,
Syngnathus acus

Size Adults range from 17–60cm

Pipefish are from the same family of fish as seahorses, Syngnathidae, with a similar shaped head. However they can be distinguished from seahorses by their long, thin body. There are six species living around the coast in shallow water and any of these may be found on the strandline for the same reasons as the seahorses. Like the seahorses, beneath their skin is an armour of bony plates which may make them unpalatable to seabirds that take them from shallow water.

Snake Pipefish,
*Entelurus
aequoreus*

Broad-nosed
Pipefish,
*Syngnathus
typhle*

Whitebait

Size Variable

Whitebait is a generic term for fish fry or small juveniles of a number of silver-coloured, shoaling fish of the herring family. These large shoals of tiny fish are preyed upon by larger fish such as Mackerel and at certain times of year may be herded into the shallows where their only escape is to leap out of the water. On occasions, the surface of the sea seems to boil as the fish are herded to the surface. Many end up stranded on the beach and can cause concern when they appear in their thousands, lining the water's edge. However, this is not a man-made problem but a natural occurrence, and offers a feeding opportunity for gulls and other coastal birds.

Occasionally larger predatory fish such as Mackerel and Horse Mackerel are found stranded on the beach which would indicate they have been chased out of the shallows by an even larger predator, perhaps a bass, shark or marine mammal.

Atlantic Mackerel *Scomber scombrus*

Size Up to 60cm
Mackerel is a fast-swimming fish with a distinctive blue-green back and zigzag markings. It is normally present in large shoals and is a staple food of many marine mammals and seabirds.

Horse Mackerel *Trachurus trachurus*

Size Up to 70cm
The Horse Mackerel is a silvery fish identified by the row of raised bony scales on either side at the rear end. It is a shoaling fish but juveniles are sometimes seen accompanying large jellyfish.

Oceanic Puffer *Lagocephalus lagocephalus*

Size Up to 61cm

Although rarely recorded as a stranding on UK shores, the Oceanic Puffer, a species of pufferfish, is easily recognised. As a defence against predation, its underside is covered in thorny spines. A further defence involves the fish taking in water and inflating its body, making it difficult for predators to eat. If all that fails, the fish also contains a deadly poison. Specimens can be found either wholly or partially inflated, or deflated.

Ocean Sunfish *Mola mola*

Size Up to 4m

The scientific name, *mola*, meaning millstone, refers to the unusual disc-shape of this fish, which has a frill rather than a tail at the rear and tall dorsal and anal fins. It is the world's heaviest bony fish and produces the most eggs of any fish – 100 million. It is a widespread oceanic fish and an infrequent summer visitor to British shores, although the individuals recorded here tend to be small, often described as dustbin-lid sized. Sunfish that stray into the Channel or North Sea in the summer may be unable to find their way back to the open ocean and it is thought that the cold shock of low winter sea temperatures may kill them, resulting in dead strandings.

Ocean Drifters

Driftwood

Wood can end up in the sea for a variety of reasons and comes in a wide range of shapes and sizes, all of which can be termed 'driftwood'. It includes uprooted trees and branches that have been washed down rivers; timbers from wooden ships and boats, broken piers and jetties; or wooden pallets and lost timber from cargo ships. Marine animals may colonise wood as it drifts in the sea or, for example with boat hulls or jetty structures, while it is *in situ*. Some wood may have been bored by insect larvae while still on land and wash ashore with the holes still intact.

Driftwood provides an attachment for a variety of animals that spend their lives drifting the ocean currents, such as goose barnacles and Columbus Crabs (see page 182). This section begins with marine animals that bore into the wood, leaving tunnels and other evidence of their presence.

DESIRABLE DRIFTWOOD

Driftwood found on the beach is often collected for its aesthetic quality and used to decorate homes and gardens, or as fire-wood. However, it is an important part of the strandline habitat, providing shelter, food and a breeding site for a number of rare and endemic strandline species whose presence is restricted by the amount of driftwood available to them on any particular beach. While sun-bleached and sea-worn driftwood can be a beautiful and tactile adornment in our homes, it should be collected in a sustainable manner, leaving plenty for the wildlife that needs it. Always check underneath for signs of inhabitants before removing it.

Shipworms Teredinidae

Above: A shipworm inside its tube

Size 50cm

There are a number of different shipworm species and a single piece of driftwood may house more than one. Despite their name, shipworms are bivalve molluscs with a small, ridged shell and an elongated soft body which is too big to be contained in the shell. The ridges on the shell are used to bore into wood, producing a tunnel which is then lined with smooth calcareous deposits to protect the animal's soft body. From within the safety of their burrows, shipworms filter seawater for nutrients. The burrows meander through the timber, mostly following the grain of the wood and leaving bold patterns. Shipworm wood is often found with the white chalky burrow linings still intact and may even contain the hinged shells.

Long-haul driftwood arriving on UK shores may bring new species not previously recorded here. The cavities created by shipworms in a timber may also provide shelter to other species and it is worth investigating these for animals such as Columbus Crabs and other ocean drifters.

The shells of shipworms

Gribble *Limnoria lignorum*

Size 5mm

'Gribble wood' is commonly found on beach strandlines but unlike the shipworm wood it is covered in a fine lattice-work of shallow, narrow tunnels. The Gribble is a species of crustacean akin to woodlice, which feeds on the timber itself, eating its way through pier legs, wooden pilings and other man-made structures in the sea, causing decay and destruction to them. As the Gribble only measures 5mm long the tunnels are much smaller than those of shipworms, and are unlined. They tend to be parallel to the surface of the wood and often so densely packed that the wood between them collapses or rots away.

Sea beans

Sea bean is the term used to describe drift seeds, designed to disperse over long distances via rivers and the sea, to wash ashore on far-flung beaches. To enable this they have hard, impermeable outer coats to prevent absorption of seawater, which would kill the seed; and some contain air pockets or other devices to provide buoyancy. They are often from tropical plants which can be common in their native country. In the past these treasures have been used as currency, for decorative pieces and as lucky charms.

Seeds found on the strandline can be from a local source, for example acorns, hazelnuts and beech mast are common on strandlines, especially if there are trees close to the beach or a stream or river enters the sea nearby. Other seeds might have been discarded on the beach by visitors, for example peach and cherry stones sometimes find their way onto strandlines. Only a small number of seeds can be termed true, long-distance sea beans, having drifted across the Atlantic from the Americas.

A drift coconut

Hazelnuts, beech mast and acorns are of local origin

Sea beans, having travelled for months, if not years, on the ocean currents, may arrive on UK shores with animals such as goose barnacles attached. Some sea beans, however, are never fouled and retain their shiny coat, possibly due to some chemical anti-fouling compound.

Here we have included a variety of sea beans including those most likely to be found in the UK and some with only one or two records, but by no means all of those that could be mentioned. For a more comprehensive coverage we recommend investing in a dedicated sea bean book (see page 298).

The seed pod of the Sea Heart, *Entada gigas*

Nickar nut seed pods on a live plant in Florida

Sea Heart *Entada gigas*

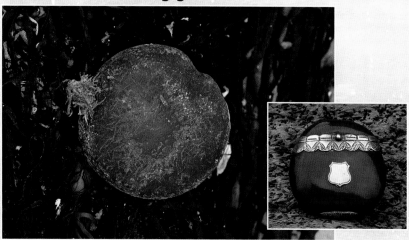

Size 6cm

This is a large sea bean, more or less circular but with an indent giving it a rounded heart-shape. It is dark to reddish-brown in colour and originates in tropical America and the West Indies. It is one of the most commonly collected sea beans, perhaps because its large size makes it easier to spot on the beach. Historically Sea Hearts have been used for a variety of personal objects including snuff boxes and vesta cases.

Nickar nuts *Caesalpinia* spp.

Nickar nuts inside their seed pod

Size 2cm

Nickar nuts, also called sea pearls, can be grey, yellowish or brown in colour depending on the species of plant that produced them. The Grey Nickar Nut is the most commonly found, although occasionally it may appear yellowish in colour. The Brown Nickar Nut is a much rarer find.

These sea beans are acorn-sized with a slightly flattened side and can float in sea water for almost 20 years. Historically, an assumed association with the Virgin Mary led to their traditional use as pain relief during childbirth.

Horse-eye beans *Mucuna* spp.

Size 2.5cm

Also called hamburger beans, this English name covers at least two different species from the *Mucuna* genus of vines found in tropical America. They are circular in shape with a flattened top and bottom. The top and bottom are coloured brown or reddish-brown with a black layer reaching almost all the way around the equator. They are some of the more commonly found sea beans on west coast UK beaches.

Sea Purse *Dioclea reflexa*

Size 3.5cm

At first glance this sea bean looks similar in colour and pattern to horse-eye beans. However, it is much flatter in shape, with a narrower central band which vaguely resembles the clasp or zip of a purse. It grows on a tropical vine in the Americas where it is dispersed by rivers and the sea and can remain afloat for at least 18 years. Sea Purses washed ashore in the UK have been successfully germinated.

Mary's Bean *Merremia discoidesperma*

Above: The indented cross mark on the top of a Mary's Bean

Right: The underside of a Mary's Bean showing the hilum

Size 2.5cm

One of the rarest sea beans and much treasured by beachcombers, the Mary's Bean is also called the Crucifixion Bean because of the indented cross marked on the top. This gives it the resemblance of a hot-cross bun in shape although it is very dark brown or black in colour. It comes from a type of beach vine which only grows in a small area of Central America.

MARY'S BEAN – FAMILY HEIRLOOM

Because of the indented cross on its surface, its assumed association with the Virgin Mary and its ability to survive the Atlantic crossing, the Mary's Bean has been carried as a protective talisman to ward off evil. Much of the folklore surrounding this bean originated in the Outer Hebrides, where beans were sometimes mounted in silver and worn as a charm, while others were clutched by women in labour to ensure an easy delivery. For this reason, treasured beans were handed down as family heirlooms from mother to daughter.

Box Fruit *Barringtonia asiatica*

Size 15cm

This relatively large and unmistakable sea bean is found as the whole fruit with the seed hidden deep inside. It is square in cross-section with a thin, papery outer covering over a fibrous inner layer. Although not native to the Atlantic coasts of the Americas it has been planted there, having originally come from mangroves in the Indian Ocean and western Pacific Ocean. Only a handful of these sea beans have, as yet, been recorded in the UK.

Sea Coconut *Manicaria saccifera*

Size 5cm

The Sea Coconut comes from a palm tree which has one of the largest leaves on Earth and grows in Central and tropical South America. It grows in swampy areas and the fruits are designed to be dispersed by water. The sea bean is round and golf-ball sized with several thin, flaky outer layers which wear away revealing the brown seed beneath.

Starnut palms *Astrocaryum* spp.

Size 4cm

These uncommon tear-shaped sea beans get their name from the star patterns etched around the three pores at the blunt end. Also called widow's tears, they are black with pale streaks that radiate from the pores to the sharp tip. These palms grow in tropical America and the West Indies.

Prickly palms *Acrocomia* spp.

Size 3.5cm

Only a handful of these sea beans have been recorded in the UK. They are circular seeds, flattened top and bottom, with three noticeable pores around the equator. Prickly palm trees are tall and grow in tropical South America and the West Indies.

Bay Bean *Canavalia maritima*

Size 2cm

These small sea beans come from a pea-like plant that grows just above the high-tide mark on tropical beaches in the Americas. Although they are produced in abundance and are able to remain afloat for many years in the sea, they are relatively rarely recorded in the UK. This may be due to their small size and brown colour which makes them blend in with other drift material on the beach. There may also be some confusion with our native acorns and hazel nuts.

Tropical Almond *Terminalia catappa*

Size 6cm

Also known as the Sea Almond, this plant has been introduced to the tropical Americas from Asia where it originated and grows by the coast. The seed is housed in a tough, fibrous coat that floats when dried and is dispersed by ocean currents. As the name suggests it resembles a large almond.

Antidote Vine *Fevillea cordifolia*

Size 5cm

This almond-like sea bean is from a climbing vine in tropical Central and South America. It contains a chemical which has been used as a laxative, to treat many ailments and as an antidote to poisoning. It is variable in shape but generally circular and flattened.

ONLY ONE

We are aware of only one record of the Antidote Vine sea bean in the UK, which was found by Dr Paul Gainey on a Cornish beach. On the same day, only 20m away, he also found a drift Coconut which had goose barnacles attached, indicating it had been on an oceanic voyage. As drift items often travel long distances together confined in a small parcel of water (see page 10), he was able to conclude that the Antidote Vine had almost certainly accompanied it.

This demonstrates that, on finding a long-distance drift item on the beach, it is certainly worth doing a thorough search in the vicinity to see if there are more.

Coconut *Cocos nucifera*

Size 30cm

Coconuts have evolved to be dispersed by ocean currents and inevitably a proportion of those stranded in the UK have travelled across the ocean. However, they are imported into Europe in huge quantities and it is highly probable that some of those found have been lost from ships while in transit. To determine whether a Coconut found on the beach is a true drift seed check that its fibrous outer husk is intact, and for signs of drift animals attached or holes bored by shipworm or other bivalve molluscs.

FRAGILE BORER

In 2014 Tracey Williams discovered a Coconut on a Cornish beach which had goose barnacles attached to the outer husk. This indicated a true drift Coconut. Further investigation by Dr Paul Gainey and David Fenwick uncovered a boring mollusc living inside which they identified as a Fragile Piddock, *Martesia fragilis;* the first record of this pelagic species in the UK. The Coconut also contained a number of shipworms, another type of boring mollusc.

The Fragile Piddock, after being extracted from the Coconut

Jellyfish

Jellyfish are simple animals that drift in the sea carried by tides and currents. Most species live in coastal waters rather than oceanic. Their swimming action is not strong enough to propel them against prevailing currents, although they can swim vertically in the water column. They tend to be in the top few metres of water, close to the surface, and as such can be driven ashore by strong winds, often resulting in mass strandings of single or mixed species.

Jellyfish belong to the group of animals called Cnidaria which also includes sea anemones, corals and hydroids. They all produce stinging cells called nematocysts which fire venom into their prey. All jellyfish sting but some are more potent than others. It is recommended not to handle ANY jellyfish, as they can continue to sting after death when stranded on the beach.

Like the caterpillar/butterfly life cycle, most jellyfish go through a number of stages during their life. Microscopic planula larvae settle to the seabed and attach to a solid structure, where they transform into a polyp (scyphistoma). Each polyp develops into a chain of polyps, which individually break away from the end of the chain as free-swimming medusas. These grow into the familiar jellyfish adults that will produce eggs and sperm and start the cycle again. In jellyfish the medusa is the dominant stage.

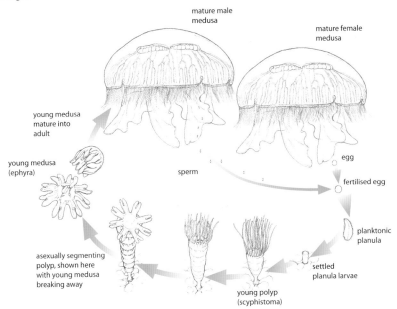

mature male medusa

mature female medusa

young medusa mature into adult

young medusa (ephyra)

sperm

egg

fertilised egg

planktonic planula

asexually segmenting polyp, shown here with young medusa breaking away

settled planula larvae

young polyp (scyphistoma)

The life cycle of the Moon Jellyfish, *Aurelia aurita*

Moon Jellyfish *Aurelia aurita*

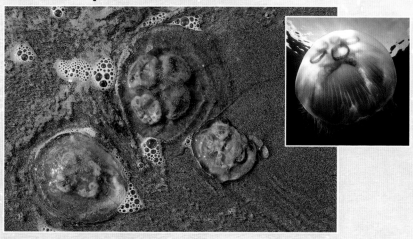

Size 35cm

Moon Jellyfish is one of the more common species and is easily recognisable by its transparent bell with (usually) four pink or purple rings which are the reproductive structures. It feeds on microscopic plankton and as such has a very mild sting.

Barrel Jellyfish *Rhizostoma pulmo*

Size 80cm

The Barrel Jellyfish, although large and robust, is a plankton-eater and has a very mild sting. There are no trailing tentacles but instead, the stinging cells are tiny and arranged in the cauliflower-like arms hanging beneath the bell.

Compass Jellyfish *Chrysaora hysoscella*

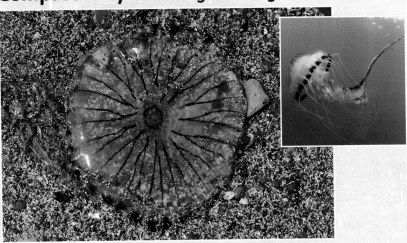

Size 30cm

The Compass jellyfish gets its name from the brown, V-shaped markings on the bell which resemble the points of a compass. The long, trailing tentacles hanging from the bell are covered in stinging cells that have a strong venom and produce a painful sting. It may be found in mixed swarms with Blue Jellyfish.

Blue Jellyfish *Cyanea lamarckii*

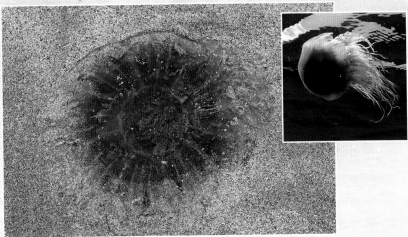

Size 30cm

The Blue Jellyfish can inflict a painful sting from the upper surface of the bell which contains clusters of stinging cells. Younger specimens may be translucent, or pale yellow and brown to light blue and purple in colour and can be confusing to identify. They are delicate and easily broken when washed ashore, usually losing the tentacles.

Mauve Stinger *Pelagia noctiluca*

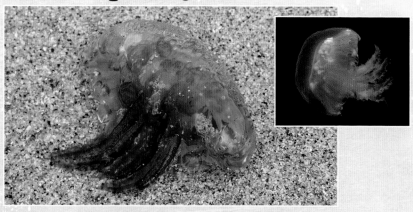

Size 12cm

This is one of the few oceanic species of British jellyfish, normally found offshore but sometimes in coastal waters in late summer. It is a small, pink or mauve jellyfish with a powerful sting. The bell is covered in warts which contain stinging cells, as do the tentacles and other parts of the jellyfish. The name '*noctiluca*' refers to the phosphorescent bell, which glows in the dark if disturbed.

Lion's Mane Jellyfish *Cyanea capillata*

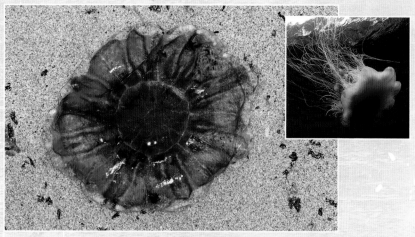

Size 50cm

A close relative of the Blue Jellyfish and similar in structure, the Lion's Mane Jellyfish is one of the largest in the world. In British waters it usually grows up to 50cm in diameter but can grow much larger in more northern latitudes. Some reports say the tentacles can stretch to over 30m long, covering a large area in which to catch potential prey, including plankton, small fish and other jellyfish. The name derives from its yellow, brown or golden colour and the mass of fine hair-like tentacles. These deliver a potent sting, made more severe by the sheer volume of stinging cells.

BIG-EYE AMPHIPOD

Some species of jellyfish, including Barrel, Compass and Moon Jellyfish, can sometimes act as hosts for a species of crustacean called the Big-eye Amphipod, *Hyperia galba*. It is parasitic, living within and feeding on the tissue of its jellyfish host, but may abandon it if washed ashore and attempt to retreat back to the sea, presumably to find another host. This amphipod measures 12mm and resembles a sandhopper, except for its very large distinctive green eyes.

Big-eye Amphipod

Hydroid medusa

Although for hydroids the dominant life-stage is the sessile, polyp stage, a number of them produce a medusa stage which resembles a jellyfish, called a hydromedusa, and occasionally these can be found on the strandline.

Many-ribbed Jellyfish *Aequorea forskalea*

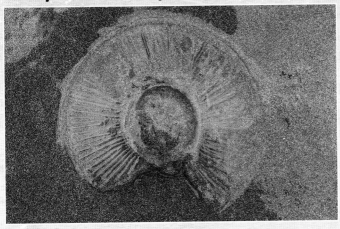

Size 17.5cm
This is one of the most likely hydroid medusae to be found on the strandline. It consists of a clear jelly bell with fine white lines radiating from a central ring. It could be mistaken for a moon jellyfish but lacks the distinctive pink or mauve rings.

Comb jellies

The scientific name for this group of planktonic carnivores is Ctenophora from the Greek words for 'Comb-bearer'. This refers to the eight rows of combs made up of beating hairs or cilia that propel the animal through the water and also give it a shimmering rainbow effect in life. Comb jellies are transparent and difficult to spot in the water, except during the summer months when they can swarm in coastal waters.

Sea Gooseberry *Pleurobrachia pileus*

Size 2cm

This small, spherical comb jelly has a pair of sticky fishing tentacles that extend into the water column to catch zooplankton and then are withdrawn into the transparent body of the animal. Sea Gooseberries can be found stranded on sandy beaches in the summer at the water's edge, looking like tiny, transparent, jelly balls. Closer inspection with a hand lens might reveal the 'combs'.

A live Sea Gooseberry, note the retracted feeding tentacles

Animals of the ocean's surface

Some animals have evolved to spend their entire lives at the ocean's surface, carried by currents and blown by the wind. Normally they would not be found close to land but sometimes strong winds may carry them inshore where they are stranded on beaches. These animals live at the interface between sea and air, partly in and partly out of the water, and are called pleuston. They have a distinctive violet and blue coloration designed to camouflage them from both above and below. Pleustonic species make up an unusual traveling community, with predatory molluscs feeding on the plankton-eaters. If one species is found on the strandline it is always worth looking out for its fellow travellers.

A mass stranding of By-the-wind Sailors

Note the erect sail and camouflaging coloration of this live Portuguese Man o'War

Portuguese Man o'War *Physalia physalis*

Size 12cm

Although often referred to as a jellyfish, this animal is really a colony of individual polyps and is a pleustonic siphonophore with the distinctive pink-tinged blue coloration. It looks like a balloon with a pink crest and long blue tentacles, reportedly stretching up to 30m in length. In strandings the tentacles are often damaged or lost, having come into contact with the seabed, but the float is usually intact. **THE TENTACLES DELIVER A POWERFUL AND VERY PAINFUL STING AND THIS ANIMAL SHOULD NOT BE TOUCHED!**

The polyps carry out individual jobs. Some will form and control the float, some the tentacles, and some are for feeding or breeding. The gas-filled float acts like a sail to catch the wind, some are right-sailing and some are left-sailing to distribute them in the ocean.

Portuguese Men o'War are normally found in tropical and sub-tropical waters and only occasionally wash up on British coasts following prolonged south-westerly winds. When they do occur it is usually as a large and widespread stranding.

At sea, the gas-filled float is flexible and can be adjusted and angled to catch the wind from whichever direction it is blowing. We once collected a stranded live specimen and put it in a tank of water. When we blew gently on it from one direction it raised and angled the crest to catch the air movement. When we blew from the other side it curled the crest in the opposite direction.

Portuguese Men o'War generally travel in a group, or as we call it, an armada. Their predators include Loggerhead Turtles, Violet Snails and Ocean Sunfish.

By-the-wind Sailor *Velella velella*

Size 6cm

Mass strandings of these small pleustonic animals are a regular occurrence on Atlantic coasts. Like the Portuguese Man o'War, they are colonial animals which form an oval disc trimmed with a blue skirt beneath which many short blue tentacles hang, and above that there is a triangular sail. They are often found fresh, still with their blue coloration, but can also be found dried in which case they appear colourless and papery. Sails can be left- or right-handed and the upper surface is water-repellent. If capsized the animal can right itself by flexing its mantle. By-the-wind Sailors normally strand in large numbers, occasionally completely covering the strandline.

Violet snails

This group of gastropods, Janthinidae, are also known as purple storm snails because of their brightly coloured, violet shells. The shell is thin and fragile, designed for floating on water, but to increase the snail's buoyancy and sailing ability it produces a mucus bubble-raft which can remain intact for some time on the strandline. The normal travelling position is with the spire of the shell pointing down in the water and the flat base uppermost. For this reason it is paler towards the spire to disguise it better against the light sky when viewed from below by predators such as young turtles. These animals travel with and prey on By-the-wind Sailors and Portuguese Men o'War. Three species have been recorded on strandlines in the UK, although rarely.

A Violet Snail floating with its bubble raft

Violet Snail *Janthina janthina*

Above: A freshly stranded Violet Snail

Size 3.5cm
Most UK records are of this species. The pale spire and darker base of the shell are very obvious and the aperture is D-shaped.

Pale Violet Snail *Janthina pallida*

Size 2.5cm

This snail has a much paler shell than the Violet Snail with a proportionately bigger aperture. Small individuals can sometimes be found on By-the-wind Sailors.

Ridged Violet Snail *Janthina exigua*

Size 1.5cm

This snail has a distinctive sculpted and ridged shell with a V-shaped notch in the aperture.

Globe Violet Snail *Janthina globosa*

Size 3.8cm

The Globe Violet Snail has a larger and slightly flared aperture and a subtle herring-bone pattern along the centre of the outer whorl. Although there are no UK records for this species, it could easily be mistaken for *J. janthina* and has the same habitat and distribution, so is worth looking out for.

Goose barnacles and associated animals

Goose barnacles are crustaceans, akin to crabs and prawns, but are more closely related to acorn barnacles found attached to rock. They are oceanic animals that attach to drifting objects at the ocean's surface where their flexible stalk or neck (peduncle) enables them to angle their feeding legs (cirri) to best effect in order to catch planktonic prey. Ocean currents and onshore winds occasionally carry them into coastal waters where they wash up onto beaches and die.

Small objects may carry single or small groups of goose barnacles but large items, such as logs or large fishing buoys, may carry many thousands. Larger colonies may also host other drift species like the Columbus Crab (page 186), *Fiona pinnata* seaslug (page 188) or the pelagic isopod *Idotea metallica* (page 188).

Several types of goose barnacle wash up on British shores, mostly on Atlantic coasts and often in mixed groups.

Conchoderma virgatum filter feeding on plankton

Common Goose Barnacle *Lepas anatifera*

Size 5cm
This is the largest and most commonly found goose barnacle in Britain. The shell plates covering the head (capitulum) are usually smooth and white.

Buoy Barnacle *Dosima fascicularis*

Size 4cm
This animal often builds its own polystyrene-like float but can also be found attached to objects such as feathers, seaweed and litter. The shell plates are thin, translucent and fragile-looking.

Lepas pectinata

Size 1.5cm
This small goose barnacle is often found with Common Goose Barnacles but is smaller with creamy-coloured, chequered shell plates. It is sometimes found on drifting seaweed.

Orange-collared Goose Barnacle *Lepas hilli*

Size 3cm
Rarely stranded in Britain, this large goose barnacle can be found with and looks similar to the Common Goose Barnacle but is easily distinguished by its orange collar and legs.

Lepas anserifera

Size 3.8cm
This goose barnacle has a chequered pattern on its shell plates similar to *Lepas pectinata* but with a white shell and yellowy-orange stalk. It is rare in Britain.

Conchoderma virgatum

Size 2.5cm
This rarely recorded animal attaches to fish, turtles and other marine animals as well as drifting objects. Its body is covered in blue-tinged stripy skin.

Rabbit-ear Barnacle *Conchoderma auritum*

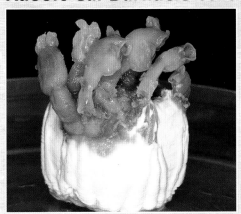

Size 2.5cm
This animal typically attaches to whale barnacles on whales, but also ship hulls and drifting objects. Its body is covered in skin with two distinguishing ear-like tubes. It is rarely recorded but most likely to be found attached to stranded cetaceans.

Columbus Crab *Planes minutus*

Size 2cm

This small, pelagic crab, sometimes called the Gulf Weed Crab, lives on flotsam floating at the ocean's surface, including rafts of Sargassum weed (see page 40), driftwood, fishing buoys and other litter. It has also been found living on Loggerhead Turtles. Its shell reflects the colour of the item it lives on and it is believed that as it grows and moults its shell progressively blends in with its background. Colour therefore varies from deep brown to olive-green or orange and can be plain, mottled or patterned with white.

Research has shown that the number of these long-distance voyagers living on an object is determined by its size. Single crabs might inhabit a fairly small drift item whereas a large log beached in Dorset was found to have 17 Columbus Crabs living inside it.

Columbus Crab larvae drift in the plankton until they find a suitable piece of flotsam to settle on. As juvenile or adult crabs they have a limited swimming ability so tend to stay with their home, venturing short distances into the blue to catch passing food. They cannot go too far, however, as if they lose their raft they are doomed either to sink to the depths or be eaten.

These extraordinary crabs have evolved for this particular nomadic lifestyle and are opportunistic feeders. They are often associated with clumps of goose barnacles, feeding on their larvae. This is, therefore, a good place to look for them on the strandline, where they may be found clinging to the base of goose barnacle stalks, especially on dense clumps.

Until 2006, when a number of Columbus Crabs were recorded on beaches in Hampshire, Dorset and Cornwall, they were believed to be extremely rare finds in the UK. However since then many more have been found, mainly on fishing buoys and equipment. This may be a result of more people looking for them and knowing where to look for them, as they are very cryptic animals and are easily overlooked. Despite having travelled thousands of miles from tropical waters in the western Atlantic ocean, these crabs often wash ashore alive and have been found living on the strandline for several days, out of water in the depths of winter.

AN EXCITING DISCOVERY

Our first Columbus Crab was found at the beginning of December 2006 when large amounts of flotsam, much of it covered in clumps of goose barnacles, was washing ashore in Dorset. Having brought home a goose barnacle-covered American fishing buoy, a live orange-and-white crab fell out and posed a bit of a mystery. Looking through our identification books, we failed to find anything that looked like this crab and resorted to phoning a friend who had a more extensive library. Dr Lin Baldock tentatively suggested it might be a Columbus Crab and further investigation confirmed this. On closer examination of the buoy it was found to be sheltering two more crabs. The excitement this discovery caused, both for ourselves and for other experienced beachcombers who subsequently were able to go out and find their own specimens, is hard to imagine. However perhaps the most exciting thing was that, having discovered these initial crabs, we were then able to go and find many more, knowing where to look for them, and even used specialist equipment to explore holes and crevices in likely drift items.

Using an endoscope to explore a driftwood cavity

A pelagic isopod *Idotea metallica*

Size 3cm

This rare isopod is known to inhabit floating Gulf Stream debris, living on the submerged parts. The individuals arriving in UK waters originate from the sub-tropical waters of the north-east coast of America, where they are widely distributed. Although records of this species have been collected off-shore in the UK, very few have been recorded from beaches. However, our records of them have all been from inside bait pots (link to fishing litter) with the lids still intact. We assume that the animals enter the pots as larvae, swimming through the tiny holes, and then develop inside, unable to escape, but usually surviving, presumably feeding on plankton and algae settling inside the pot. Carefully unscrewing the lids of the easily recognisable bait pots will sometimes reveal what look like small woodlice living in the bottom. These could be *Idotea metallica* or another isopod species, almost certainly having travelled here in the Gulf Stream.

Fiona pinnata

Size 2cm

This sea slug is an ocean wanderer, travelling with and feeding on goose barnacles and By-the-wind Sailors. Its colour depends on which animals it has been feeding on, brown for goose barnacles and blue for By-the-wind Sailors. It lives in tropical oceans around the world and has only very rarely been found stranded in the UK.

Exotic non-natives on marine litter

Man-made objects found on the beach may sometimes be colonised by marine animals and investigation of these may reveal that they are not native to our shores. If goose barnacles are attached this immediately tells us that the item has drifted here from the open ocean and may even have travelled from distant shores. Animals may have settled on the object while it was trapped on the seabed, or as larvae drifting in the surface waters. With the enormous increase in marine litter over the last few decades, some scientists believe the potential for new species arriving and possibly colonising in the UK has greatly increased.

While the animals in this section have only recently been recorded for the first time in the UK, we would encourage beachcombers to investigate potential long-haul objects, as rare finds such as these may become more frequent. A bit of internet searching and detective work might turn up an extremely rare find, although identification to species level is not always possible and expert help might be needed.

The Gulf Stream

For beachcombers interested in the exotic animals and long-haul litter that arrives on the seashores of northern Europe, a basic understanding of the Gulf Stream may be helpful. One of the best known of all the oceanic currents, it is like a huge river running across the North Atlantic Ocean from Florida, travelling north along the eastern coast of the USA before veering offshore towards Europe. Despite the term 'Stream', this current carries more water in it than all the land-sourced rivers that flow into the Atlantic Ocean. It can measure 100km across and more than 1km deep, travelling at around 8.8km per hour or 209km a day at its fastest.

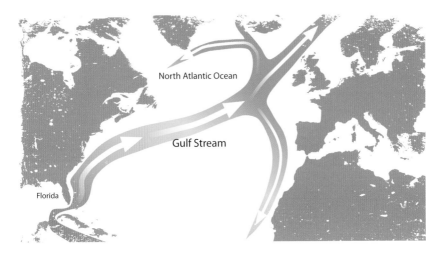

North Atlantic Ocean

Gulf Stream

Florida

Once over deep water in the middle of the ocean the stream splits, sending some water north-east towards the British Isles and Norway, and some south-east towards North Africa where it then turns west again as the North Equatorial Current. This travels back across the Atlantic to the Caribbean and Florida, completing the circle. This clockwise circulation of water is called the North Atlantic Subtropical Gyre and the Gulf Stream forms its northern part. There are 11 major oceanic gyres in the world, some circulating clockwise and others anti-clockwise. Smaller currents and eddies link up the gyres and in theory, if timing was right and conditions were suitable, a drifting object could circumnavigate the globe using these gyres.

The North Atlantic Drift, the northward of the two currents, is the part of the Gulf Stream that brings long-haul litter to our shores and is commonly thought to be responsible for our mild climate. Depending on the position of the jet stream and weather conditions, the Gulf Stream tends to meander and its exact course is variable. This could result in the irregular amounts of beachcombing finds we see from year to year, even on the same beach.

Pearl Oyster *Pinctada imbricata* and
Purse Oyster *Isognomon bicolor*

Pearl Oyster, left, and Purse Oyster, right

Oyster embedded in a longline drum

Size 10cm

Both these species were found attached to the same item of fishing gear. They use byssus threads to attach themselves to a variety of underwater substrates including soft corals and mangrove roots. On this occasion they settled on a plastic item of litter which carried them to the UK where they had not been recorded before. The shells have a flaky, layered structure and they are angular in shape with a straight hinge.

Jingle shells Anomiidae

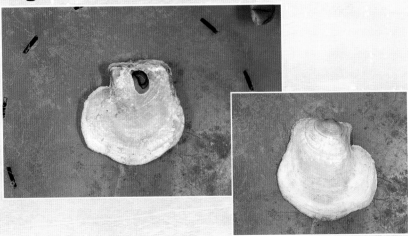

Size 5cm

Jingle shell is the group name given to the many species of saddle oysters often found on flotsam. They are small, paper-thin shells and the bottom valve has a hole through which the byssus threads attach to the drift object. Sometimes hundreds of them can be found on a single fish box or other flat object. Identification to species level is notoriously difficult but undoubtedly some of these species have travelled across the Atlantic.

Jewel box clams Chamidae

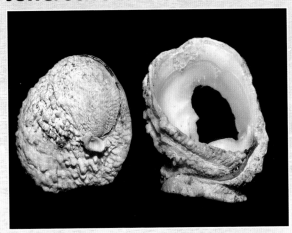

Size up to 8cm

Also known as chamas, these chalky, bivalve mollusc shells have a lower half that is box or cup-shaped with the flat top half acting like a lid. They have been found on two occasions attached within the handle of a fish box. The animals mould their shells to the contours of their substrate or host object.

Stone coral *Astrangia* spp.

Size Variable

The white, stony skeleton of this hard coral was found attached to part of a crab trap used in the USA. The fact that this coral is unlike any UK species in form, and also that it was attached to a type of fishing gear not used here, indicated that this was a non-native species.

Caprella andreae

Size 1cm

This small crustacean, vaguely resembling a praying mantis, can be found clinging to algae, hydroids or bryozoans growing on flotsam, including fishing buoys and coconuts. It can be seen to 'rear up', swaying and lifting its front legs. These animals are very rarely recorded in the UK, however, being small and cryptic they are easily overlooked. Expert identification is needed to determine species as they belong to a group containing some commonly found species.

Jassa marmorata

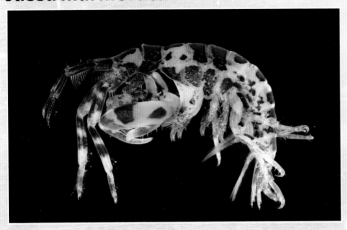

Size 1cm

This small amphipod is found living on rafts of floating debris, buoys and the like, and occurs in the North Atlantic but has also been introduced to many countries around the world. Exact distribution is unclear as it has only recently been distinguished from *Jassa falcata*. It has been found in the UK on an American fishing buoy which also carried Columbus Crabs (page 186) and *Caprella andreae* (opposite).

Frond Oyster *Dendostrea frons*

Size Up to 7.5cm

This is a bivalve mollusc belonging to the oyster family. It moulds its shell to attach to its chosen substrate, as is typical of oysters, although for the Frond Oyster this often results in a distinctive, claw-like projection on the back of the shell which wraps around structures such as ropes, seafans and sea whips. The two valves can have an exaggerated zigzag-shaped rim where they close. It is found around the Gulf coast of North America and the Caribbean.

Zigzag Scallop *Euvola ziczac*

Size 7.5cm

This bivalve exhibits the familiar scallop shape. It is normally found living on the seabed in the shallow tropical waters of Bermuda and the Caribbean. However, it has been recorded inside a North American bait (Scotty) pot along with another type of tropical scallop, *Aequipecten heliacus*, presumably both having entered as larvae on the western side of the Atlantic and developed inside the pot as it was carried east to the UK. The Zigzag Scallop is so-named either because of the zigzag markings visible on its shell or after its erratic swimming style, moving in a zigzag path to escape predators.

Aequipecten heliacus

Atlantic Wing Oyster *Pteria colymbus*

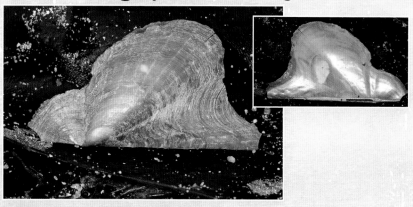

Size up to 9cm

This bivalve mollusc has an asymmetrical shape with one valve much smaller than the other, and one small triangular 'wing' and one elongated. Each valve has one, long, straight side where they join at the hinge. It is found on Gulf coasts of North America, the Caribbean and northern South America where it attaches, using byssus threads, to seafans and algae, or hard structures.

Pen shells *Atrina* spp.

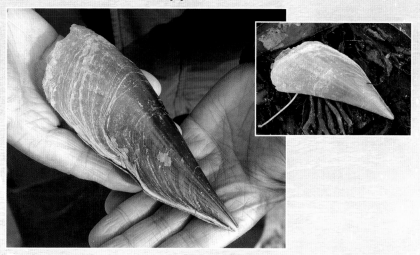

Size up to 28cm

This group of large bivalves belong to the Pinnidae family of molluscs, related to mussels and producing similar byssus threads by which they attach to hard substrates buried beneath sand or mud. There are several American species, which closely resemble our native Fan Mussel, *Atrina fragilis;* golden-brown in colour and with a very thin, delicate shell. Although they are normally buried in soft sediment they have been found attached to large, drifting objects.

Pebbles with a difference

Amber

Some UK beaches occasionally collect pieces of amber, especially on the east and south-east coasts of England. Amber was formed from the resin which oozed from long dead pine trees. A forest of these trees once grew where the Baltic Sea now lies, and this is thought to be the source of the amber which washes up today.

Occasionally the amber pebbles have 'inclusions' where small insects or plant material became trapped in the sticky resin before it hardened. These may be revealed if the amber is polished. Pebbles of amber found on the beach are yellow or golden in colour and feel light, like a piece of plastic. They are not necessarily shiny like the amber found in jewellery.

Jet

Jet is formed from the fossilised wood of a type of monkey puzzle tree, which was abundant in the Jurassic era. Trees carried down rivers into the sea sank to the seafloor where over millennia they were buried in mud and fossilised. Jet is found in thin seams in Jurassic-age rocks and has been used for thousands of years to make jewellery and ornaments. The best place to look for it is on coastlines with this age of rock.

When found on the beach, jet 'pebbles' are hard, shiny and 'jet-black' in colour. They feel light and look and sound (when tapped) like a piece of hard plastic.

Pumice

Above: aerated cement block

Pumice is a type of volcanic rock, ejected from erupting volcanoes on land, or on the seafloor by underwater eruptions. It is pale grey in colour and rough in texture, filled with a matrix of bubbles and sometimes containing crystals. The bubble-filled texture of the rock causes it to float in water and, in volcanic regions, pebbles or larger lumps of pumice commonly wash ashore on beaches.

Occasionally pumice can be found on UK beaches, having been carried here by ocean currents. However, some types of man-made building blocks can be mistaken for pumice if they have been rounded and worn on a beach. Real pumice can be identified by its irregular bubble-matrix, as opposed to the very regular texture of man-made blocks. The presence of crystals and attached animals such as goose barnacles is another good indication of volcanic pumice.

Sea glass

Sea glass comes in a wide variety of colours and shapes – colourless, green, blue and brown are the most commonly found. Depending on how long it has been rolling around on the beach or seafloor it can be angular and clear or, if it is well worn, rounded and frosted. The glass can come from a variety of sources, such as bottles, jars and old-style fishing buoys.

Sea glass collecting can be an addictive pastime and some colours and shapes are much sought after. The old style glass bottle stoppers and the button-shaped seals from the inside of glass fishing buoys are collectors' items. The more rounded and frosted a piece of sea glass, the more desirable it is, and these sea-worn items are sometimes called Mermaid's Tears.

FUN WITH SEA GLASS

Sea glass, shells and pebbles collected from the beach plus a sprinkling of imagination can provide a great activity, especially after a beach walk on a blustery day. Creating an artistic arrangement of your finds on a flat piece of driftwood, a canvas or even a piece of cardboard is a satisfying way to spend an hour or so. Whether crafting sea creatures, designing Christmas decorations or just organising your finds in a jar or dish, you can produce personal ornaments for your home that fill it with happy memories of beachcombing.

Marine and beach litter

The rise of plastic

Until the latter part of the 20th century, any man-made objects floating in the sea or deposited on beaches were mostly made of natural materials – wood, paper, cloth, rubber, with some glass in the form of bottles and fishing floats. Even fishing pots and nets were made from willow and hemp.

However, the introduction of plastic in its many different forms changed everything, and its longevity made it a very attractive product. Plastics were soon being used in every aspect of our daily lives. The consequence of this is that plastic and plastic-derived products inevitably end up in the sea, either accidentally or through deliberate dumping.

Official reports suggest some 8 million items of marine litter are being dumped in oceans and seas every day, amounting to about 6.4 million tonnes per year.

The rise of litter

Alongside this increase in the variety of plastic materials, we have developed into a society of rampant consumerism. Many of the items we rely on are disposable, to be used once and discarded – we have become a 'throw-away' society. It is ironic that we use a material that will last indefinitely to make a product with a very short life-span.

How does litter enter the sea?

There are a number of recognised routes through which litter enters the sea, some accidental and others deliberate.

Fishing

Fishing equipment is often lost while in the sea, for example crab pots left on the seabed may be lost in a storm and fishing nets may be caught on wreckage. Items can also be accidentally washed overboard from fishing vessels in rough weather. However, broken items are often deliberately discarded into the sea. Most fishing litter is easy to identify and these objects are among the most common items found on beach strandlines.

Shipping

On the high seas it is all too easy to dispose of rubbish overboard despite international laws which seek to prevent this. Everyday litter such as drinking-water bottles, cigarette lighters and food packaging is frequently discarded overboard. Among the regular items washed up on beaches are the consumables used by ships and other vessels, such as water filters, man-overboard beacons, oil drums, bilge cleaner bottles and grease tubes. In addition to this, shipping is the major form of transport for the distribution of products and every year an estimated 10,000 shipping containers are lost overboard from ships.

Some of the millions of packets of cigarettes lost from a container ship in 2014

A famous lost shipping container contained 28,800 plastic bath toys, including the now famous ducks which for many years afterwards continued to wash ashore all around the world. Shipping containers hold everyday items which wash onto our beaches, sometimes in very large numbers. So when you find a toothbrush or a child's toy on the beach, it may not have entered the sea from land but could have been cargo from a lost shipping container.

Land-sourced litter

Much of the litter found on beach strandlines has originated from the land, either left behind by careless beach visitors or washed into rivers and carried into the sea that way.

For example, a cigarette butt casually thrown from a car window can be washed into a road-side drain by rainwater, entering a waterway which carries it into the sea. Equally, litter overflowing from a bin or skip near a river can be blown into the waterway, or spilled items in a factory may be hosed into drains. Seaside resorts can be a major source of litter, especially in the tourist season when people are eating and drinking outside, often using plastic cups or polystyrene take-away containers which are not disposed of carefully enough. All of these are routes for litter to make its way from the land into the sea.

Sewage-related debris

Another route for land-sourced litter worthy of a separate mention is via the sewage system. Items flushed down toilets frequently make their way into the sea or onto our beaches. Cotton bud sticks are a frequent find on beaches, the central plastic stick being thin enough to fit through filters in the system. Shockingly, a wider variety of sanitary waste such as plastic tampon applicators, condoms and sanitary towels are regularly seen on some beaches, especially following heavy rain. Many of our sewage systems have a mechanism to cope with large quantities of rain water. These are called Combined Sewer Overflows or CSOs (below). When heavy rain floods the sewage system

a mechanism is in place to divert it out through the CSOs to prevent flooding further up the system. CSOs exit directly onto beaches, into rivers, estuaries and the sea. Raw, untreated sewage and anything else that has been flushed down the toilet can therefore end up in the sea and on the strandline.

The global picture

Ocean gyres cover major parts of the sea area on Earth. They are rotating bodies of water driven by ocean currents. The currents circulating at the outer edge of a gyre move more quickly than those nearer the middle and floating objects can eventually make their way to the slowly moving centre, where they collect. The result is that for several decades large patches of floating debris, mostly man-made plastic items, have been growing at the centres of the world's ocean gyres. Oceanographer Curt Ebbesmeyer coined the name 'garbage patches' in the 1990s, a term which has stuck. Although items are mostly floating beneath the surface and consisting of small fragments, garbage patches have a very high concentration of plastic waste and cover vast areas. Occasionally, variations in the ocean currents can cause parts of the garbage patch to escape, carrying the litter to distant shores. Research suggests that around 70% of marine litter sinks to the seabed.

Plastic in the sea

Plastic products do not generally biodegrade, that is to say they are not broken down into organic matter that can be recycled into the environment. Over time they may be broken up into smaller fragments and eventually into a type of plastic dust. These minute pieces are called micro-plastics and have been found to be ingested by detritus and filter-feeding marine animals and thus enter the food-chain. Small plastic fragments floating in the sea are known to attract pollutants in the seawater, which stick

to the surface of the plastic making the fragment more toxic than the seawater surrounding it.

Even items that are biodegradable take much longer to degrade in seawater than they do in soil or in a pile of seaweed on the beach, making it difficult to determine how long they actually persist in the sea.

Economic cost of marine litter

Current levels of marine and beach litter result in huge economic costs to landowners, councils, farmers, fishermen and industry each year. In the United Kingdom alone, the cost to authorities, industry and coastal communities of cleaning up marine litter amounts to approximately £17.5 million per annum.

Problems for wildlife

It is estimated that around the world each year, marine litter causes the deaths of 1 million seabirds and 100,000 marine mammals and turtles. Problems arise when air-breathing animals such as turtles, birds, seals and dolphins become entangled in fishing net and line underwater and drown, or are cut, maimed or killed when they become tightly bound by rope and line. In addition, marine animals have been feeding at the

This Spurdog, *Squalus acanthias*, is protected by law, but is still very vunerable to marine litter

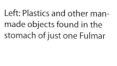

sea's surface for millions of years but it is only recently that this behaviour has resulted in ingestion of non-organic material and a potentially lethal meal. Research carried out between 2003 and 2007 found that 95% of Fulmars in the North Sea had plastic items in their stomachs.

Grey Triggerfish in the Azores using marine debris as shelter in the open ocean

It is well known that fish in the open ocean are attracted to floating objects on the surface, which provide a degree of cover and shelter in an otherwise open expanse of water. The fishing industry takes advantage of this in some instances by deliberately putting floating structures in the sea called Fish Aggregating Devices (FADs) to attract ocean-going pelagic fish such as tuna and marlin. Often large floating rafts form naturally, a mixture of natural debris such as seaweed and man-made litter. Inevitably these will attract fish beneath them and we believe that they also attract seabirds and marine mammals into this hazardous environment to feed on the fish, running the gauntlet of becoming entangled or ingesting the litter.

A WHALE OF A PROBLEM

In 2013 a dead, beached Sperm Whale was found to have 17.5 kilos of plastic, amounting to 59 items ranging from plastic sheeting and hose pipes to rope, plastic bags and flower pots, blocking its stomach. Unfortunately this is not an unusual occurrence. Among a long list of whale species possibly killed by marine litter was a Bryde's Whale in Australia in 2000 with a stomach tightly packed with supermarket carrier bags, food containers and bin bags, and a Grey Whale in Seattle in 2010 with a stomach containing clothing, surgical gloves, carrier bags and a golf ball.

Sperm Whale, *Physeter macrocephalus*, preparing for a dive

Gulls feeding amongst rafts of marine debris and litter

Litter as a form of transport

Some animals have evolved to attach to objects floating in the ocean. For millions of years they have been more or less restricted to logs, seaweed, feathers and, in human history, wooden boats. These floating objects are also known to have been a route for species to spread around the coast and colonise remote islands. However, with the huge growth of synthetic floating items entering the sea, the opportunity for attachment has greatly increased. Goose barnacles and their community may be among the very few animals that benefit from this and it has also been suggested that an increase in the number of non-native species being dispersed around the world may result.

Marine and beach litter is a huge topic and the variety of items that can be found on the strandline is limitless. The following pages focus on the types of litter most commonly found and those with a particular story to tell. Much research has been carried out on the effects of different types of marine litter in the environment and if you want to know more there is a wealth of information to be found on the internet.

THE TWO-MINUTE BEACH CLEAN

Have you had a good time at the beach? Got two minutes to spare to show your appreciation? More and more people are spending just two minutes each time they visit the beach removing litter, which can then be recycled or dropped in a bin. You can help inspire others to do the same by taking a photo of your haul and posting on Twitter or Instagram with the hashtag #2minutebeachclean. You could even make something arty with your collection. If everyone made a small difference we could all make a BIG difference! Find out more at www.beachclean.net

Fishing litter

From years of observation (and subsequent research) both above and below the water, we have found that the fishing industry is one of the most prolific sources of marine litter. Fishing gear from around the Atlantic is mixed in with that from local fisheries and one of the easiest ways to tell long-haul from UK litter is if it is fouled with goose barnacles. These animals do not breed in UK waters so encrusted items must have come from the open ocean or warmer seas. Here we have focused on long-haul litter, with the aim of helping beachcombers identify specific designs of foreign fishing gear. A bit of internet detective work will often reveal more information about an item and the fishery in which it is used. Look for manufacturers' marks or individual owners' names on gear and the more time you spend beachcombing the quicker you will learn to recognise particular items. Once you have identified an item as 'long-haul' it is worth closer inspection for exotic marine life (see page 189).

Ghost fishing is the term used for lost fishing gear in the sea which continues to trap and kill animals. Dead animals already caught attract scavengers, which in turn become trapped and die, and so the cycle continues indefinitely. The material used in modern-day nets and pots is manufactured to last and has superseded the traditional, natural materials of the past. Ghost fishing is recognised as a huge problem worldwide and in some fisheries attempts are being made to limit the life of lost gear. Examples include shellfish traps in North America with escape hatches held on by sacrificial metal rings, designed to rust and fall off if not replaced regularly, or those made of wood which will biodegrade over time.

Research has found that annually an estimated 640,000 tonnes of fishing gear is left in the world's oceans. A single fishery in the north-east Atlantic reported losing or discarding around 25,000 nets, measuring a total length of 1,250km (778 miles), each year.

Traditional biodegradable willow lobster pot

Octopus pots

A number of countries around the Atlantic Ocean and Caribbean Sea use special pots for trapping octopuses, including Morocco in North Africa and Mexico in Central America. The pots are easily identified, made of black or grey plastic with a flat, weighted bottom and a round entrance. Octopuses like to find a hole or crevice to hide in and are attracted to the pots when they are laid on the seabed. These pots are not used by any countries bordering the north-east Atlantic so when they wash ashore on UK beaches it is clear that they have travelled across the ocean. Some Moroccan pots are branded and can be traced back to source. These have been found on beaches in the UK, presumably having lost their weight, floating to the surface and being carried across the ocean to North America, from where they have been picked up in the Gulf Stream and brought to our shores.

Longline light sticks

Light sticks, also called glow-sticks or snap lights, are often found on beaches and are used by anglers, divers and commercial fishermen. They are activated by bending the stick, allowing two chemicals to mix and react together producing a glow. Fishermen use them at night, attracting squid and fish. Long-line fishing is a method used to catch species such as marlin, swordfish, tuna and other large predatory fish by paying out baited hooks on a line that can be up to 100km long. These lines can carry thousands of hooks and light sticks and inevitably many are lost at sea.

Longline hook trays

A longline hook tray resembles a large, plastic colander with a line of foam, square in cross-section, around the rim. It is used to store longline hooks. When a longline is retrieved, the hooks are unclipped from the line and hooked into the foam for storage, ready for re-baiting. The lengths of black, or yellow foam, which

are replaced regularly, are often found on strandlines, while the complete hook trays are less frequently found.

Mussel discs and pegs

Farmed mussels are grown on vertical ropes hanging in the sea. The dense clusters of grown mussels can be very heavy so plastic discs and pegs are inserted into the rope at intervals to act like shelves and bear the weight of the mussels above, preventing them from sliding down the rope. The pegs are commonly used in the UK but the discs, which bear the name Penn Cove Shellfish Company, are likely to be from North America.

Mussel pegs

Lobster and cod tags

Coloured plastic security seals or tags are often found on the strandline. Most enter the sea from ships and cannot be traced. However, there are an assortment of tags to be found which originate from the fishing industry and display a variety of types of information about their use. Here are a couple of examples but an internet search using the code on the tag may reveal more information.

Those tags used by the fishing industry in Canada are distinctive and display a series of numbers and letters, indicating the species, year and country of origin. In Canada, lobster fishermen have a limit on the number of traps they can use and each year are issued with

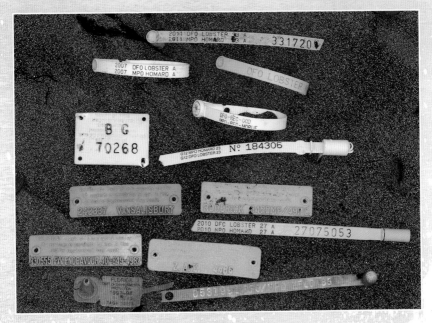

plastic tags to attach to their traps so that this can be monitored by the Department of Fisheries and Oceans (DFO). These tags usually have DFO LOBSTER and sometimes the year, usually written in English and French. They also use gill tags on cod that are sometimes caught after the quota has been filled, which means they can land the fish rather than discard it dead but that it will have no economic value. These tags display DFO-REC-COD, also in French.

Another type of crab trap tag is used in the USA and consists of an orange, rectangular label, usually with the name of the boat imprinted. These are hung inside the pot or riveted to the central stick on the pot-marker.

Finding dated tags can give an indication of how long they take to travel to the UK. It is likely that tags entering the sea in Canada first travel south along the North American coast, until they meet the Gulf Stream and are carried across the ocean to the UK.

Fish sorting conveyor belt

These white plastic items are commonly found on the strandline and may be found as individual pieces or small, linked sections and rarely as a complete conveyor belt. They are used inside fishing boats to sort fish into species and sizes and therefore unlikely to be lost accidentally. They are regularly colonised by small goose barnacles and are therefore worth investigating.

Fishing nets

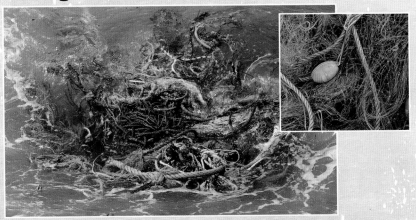

Fishing net falls into two main types – green (and blue) trawl net, and colourless monofilament net. Trawl net is made of thick, heavy duty mesh, used to haul up tons of fish onto a boat. Huge mounds of it can wash ashore, mixed in with other types of discarded fishing gear, buoys, ropes and driftwood, or smaller sections may be found that have been cut out during repair work, net in tiny fragments is among the most common types of litter found on any beach. Monofilament net (inset) is much finer, made of single plastic threads designed to be invisible underwater. It is left in place, suspended in the water column, for animals to swim into and become entangled, later being retrieved (see page 210).

Gloves and boots

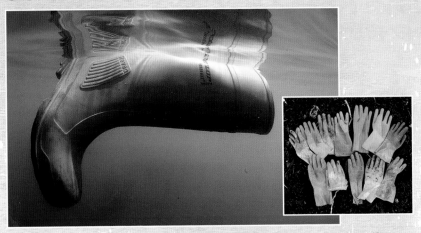

Rubber gloves and wellington boots are common finds on the strandline and most will have come from the fishing industry. The boots, often insulated, are worn when working in ice-stores or in cold conditions on commercial fishing vessels, while the tough gloves are used to protect hands when landing gear onto boats. Both are used in such huge numbers that it is inevitable that discarded items, having reached the end of their useful life, wash ashore on our beaches.

Lobster and crab trap parts

Escape vents

In North America, shellfish fishermen insert special escape vents in their traps to allow any undersized animals to escape. These plastic vents are attached to the trap by a metal ring that over time, rusts away in the sea. The fishermen must replace the rings regularly but if the trap is lost on the seabed the rings will rust and break, releasing the vent and allowing any animals inside, even large ones, to escape.

Bait pots or jars

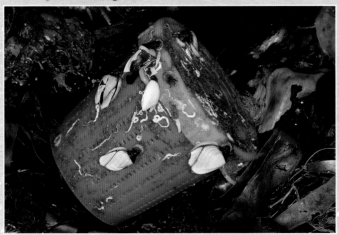

These plastic orange, screw-top bait pots are commonly found on UK beaches and are easily identified. We call them Scotty Pots, the manufacturer's name. They are used to hold bait in crab and lobster traps in parts of the USA. The pots are covered in tiny holes to allow the smell of the bait to leach out but prevent animals eating it. Sometimes they are found with the lid still screwed on and can offer an amazing opportunity to observe animals from the other side of the Atlantic Ocean that have entered as larvae and then grown inside the shelter of the pot, too large to escape. These animals, including the pelagic isopod, *Idotea metallica* (see page 188), bivalve molluscs that would normally settle on the seabed and goose barnacles, are often still alive when found on the beach. Think of these pots as a type of 'space capsule' carrying their passengers from one continent to another!

Plastic Stone Crab traps

Bait box

Stone Crab, *Menippe mercenaria*, is fished around Florida, the Caribbean and Gulf of Mexico using plastic traps, and parts of these sometimes wash up in the UK. The lids that hold the entry funnel have Florida Traps Inc. imprinted on them. Other parts include the funnels, bait cups and the small, plastic lid-latches. These are attached via a corrodible nail, so if the trap is lost, the nail will rust away releasing the latch and allowing the lid to open, thus preventing ghost-fishing.

Trap funnels

Trap catches

GARDEN MAKEOVER

The colour and variety of fishing buoys found on beaches make them immensely desirable and seaside homes often sport a display of those collected by the owner. Gathering beached buoys and other fishing debris is great for giving your garden a coastal theme, while at the same time removing litter from the beach.

An old, broken lobster pot makes a decorative planter

Fishing buoys, buffs and fenders

Fishing buoys, buffs and fenders come in many shapes, sizes and colours and have an equally wide variety of uses, from marking strings of shellfish pots, to identifying boat moorings and providing buoyancy for fishing nets and longlines. Some are designed to be seen from the surface, while others are used to suspend nets underwater. However, remember that many buoys can be used for other types of fishing than those for which they were designed and are often found by fishermen and used second-hand. Different countries may use their own types of buoys and many are marked with a boat name or number which means that some can be traced back to the region, or indeed the fisherman, from where they came. For this reason, a fishing buoy found on a beach can reveal its story if you know what to look for.

Trawl floats

These are among the most commonly found type of buoy, used by trawlers all over the world. They are made of hard plastic and are designed to be very hard-wearing for use in a tough environment. Most common colours are yellow and orange. They may be found with the green

219

trawl net they were attached to and are used to hold the mouth of the net open underwater as it is pulled through the sea.

A new style of deep-sea trawl float (opposite) looks similar to a large golf ball with dimples on the surface. These have been designed to be more hydrodynamic as the dimples create a better flow, so that the buoy offers less resistance when being towed through the water.

Vintage fishing buoys

Sometimes old-style metal or even, very occasionally, glass fishing buoys can be found. The latter will be missing their original net covering which would have biodegraded over the years. These should be treasured and in some cases are sought after by collectors.

Gill net floats and buoys

Gill or tangle nets are fine, monofilament nets set underwater to form an invisible wall to catch fish. They are weighted at the bottom with a string of small floats along the top to make the net hang vertically in the water. There are a variety of different types of float made from either hard plastic or polystyrene but they are usually oval or egg-shaped and relatively small in size.

Longline buoys

Longline fishing is a method where a single length of fishing line with hundreds or even thousands of secondary lines, each with a baited hook, are arranged along it at intervals. These can be set at various depths in the ocean and left for a period before being retrieved. Buoys are used along the line to hold it at the right depth and are sometimes called deepwater floats. These buoys tend to be smaller than trawl buoys but made from the same hard plastic so they do not compress at depth. Most common colours are green and pink and some are marked with the depth they can be used at.

To enable the line to be retrieved, large, surface-marker buoys are attached to each end of the long-line and designed to be highly visible. A variety of types of marker buoy are used for this purpose. One type is inflatable, oval-shaped and colourful, often with the boat's name hand-written on it. Another is a hard plastic buoy, often with reflective tape, with a metal screw-fitting at the top to hold a flashing strobe so it can be found at night. Bullet buoys are bullet-shaped, foam buoys tied with thick monofilament line, often with the boat name and number branded into them.

High flyers

If fishing off-shore, a surface-buoy marking fishing nets or pots below the surface must be highly visible from a distance, as it could easily be lost in the trough of a large wave. High flyers are designed to stand up vertically in the water, having a weighted base and a tall pole with a flag, strobe or aluminium radar reflector on the top. The foam buoy or pair of buoys, skewered on the pole may be cylindrical or bullet-shaped.

Buffs and fenders

Inflatable buoys, buffs and fenders are among the most commonly found on beaches and come in a variety of sizes, shapes and colours and are used in a wide variety of applications, from protecting boats at the quayside to marking shellfish pots and fishing nets. They are not necessarily from the fishing industry, although some are marked with the boat's name.

American shellfish pot buoys

Foam, bullet-shaped buoys, often painted in two colours and with a number branded onto the bottom or side, have probably come from America where they are commonly used in the shellfish potting industry. They can have a plastic stick pushed into the middle of the buoy to aid retrieval.

LEFT vs RIGHT COLLECTING BEACHES

The wind has an influence on the direction that all floating, drifting objects take, and even slight differences in the shapes of objects tend to send them off on slightly different paths, and similar-shaped objects often end up on the same beaches. It has even been found that left and right shoes and gloves are likely to drift in slightly different directions, with the result that some beaches collect more left shoes or gloves than right ones. This sorting by the ocean is sometimes reflected in the names of beaches, for example in Costa Rica there is a Sandal Beach, Toy Beach and Bottle Beach. As a fun addition to a beach clean the numbers of left and right handed shoes, boots or gloves could be compared over a year to find out if the beach in question is a left or right collecting beach.

Other common fishing finds

Much of the fishing litter found on a beach could be of local origin, from complete shellfish pots and fish boxes to individual parts. They will have been lost on the seabed and may be fouled with a variety of marine organisms and seaweed, including acorn barnacles, keel worms, saddle oysters and bryozoans. Some commonly used items are instantly recognisable, such as the entrance funnels from crab pots and the black plastic hooks used to hold the door closed. Other items may pose more of a mystery. The white figure of eight-shaped objects are pot swivels, used to prevent ropes getting entangled on strings of pots. The blue pot locks are used on some traps to allow animals in through the funnel but prevent them going back out.

Lobster pot hook

Pot funnel and lock

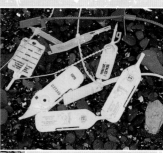

Fishery and cargo tags

Lobster inkwell pots

Fish box

Fishing pot rope swivel

Shipping litter

Nurdles

Tiny plastic pellets, also known as nurdles, are the first stage in the production of any plastic product. They appear in a range of colours and can vary slightly in shape but most are cylindrical or disc-shaped. Plastic is transported to manufacturers in this form to be melted and moulded into an astonishing range of products, from drainpipes to CDs and plastic bags to fishing equipment. They either enter the sea directly when lost by the container-load during transportation by ship, or indirectly via waterways from the manufacturer. Careless handling of this product has resulted in nurdles washing ashore on tidelines all around the world.

Nurdles are most visible on sandy beaches where they can be present as a clear line along the tide mark. On the strandline they can wash ashore in huge numbers, floating in with other debris on the water as the tide comes in, or stuck to seaweed washed up on the beach. In 2007 at least one container load was lost from the MSC *Napoli* which was deliberately grounded on the south coast of England, and in the following weeks and months they washed ashore in their billions, covering the beaches in what looked like hailstones.

The problem nurdles cause in the environment is that as they float on the sea's surface or lie on the strandline they are easily mistaken for food by animals that feed there. Tube-nosed seabirds such as Fulmars, which feed at the sea's surface, are particularly vulnerable to ingesting these items. With more nurdles entering the sea every year and none disappearing, the problem is increasing year on year.

Water filter cartridges

A commonly found strandline item that can pose a mystery is the water filter cartridge used on ships and sailing vessels. The cylindrical filters look like spools of twine but are a consumable in water filtration systems and are replaced regularly.

Man overboard beacons

These are floating devices that are thrown overboard to mark the position when a boat goes down or a life-raft is deployed. They have a radio transmitter, lights or smoke emitters to aid rescuers.

THE INCREDIBLE VOYAGE OF THE TOY DUCK

In January 1992, a shipping container carrying 28,800 bath toys was lost over board from a cargo vessel in the mid-Pacific Ocean. Thanks to eminent oceanographer, Curtis Ebbesmeyer, who has tracked these toys for more than 20 years, they have helped researchers to understand better than ever the way ocean currents circulate around all of the world's oceans, the speed they move at and how they transport objects along coasts and between continents.

The toys, made by a company called The First Years Inc., were packed in sets of four, each containing a beaver, frog, turtle and duck. Using computer modelling, Ebbesmeyer predicted where and when the toys would wash ashore and then set about finding if he was right. Sure enough, beachcombers along the west coast of North America began finding the toys more or less as predicted. Press articles and scientific papers followed and a network of devoted beachcombers was formed, providing essential data on the toys' journey around the Pacific Ocean and beyond. As a result the toys, in particular the ducks, captured the imagination of beachcombers around the world and they became a sought-after item.

Not all of the toys took the same path and while some continued to circulate around the North Pacific, completing each circuit in roughly three years, others escaped north through the Bering Strait into the Arctic Ocean. Frozen in sea ice, they moved slowly eastwards towards the North Atlantic. Eight years after the spill the first bath toys were found on the east coast of North America, taking another three years to reach the UK. Even after 16 years, drifting 34,000 miles and being frozen in sea ice the ducks were still recognisable, although faded from yellow to white.

Land-sourced litter

Balloons

Left: weather balloon
Above: foil balloon
Below: latex balloons

Balloons cause a very specific problem to marine animals and for this reason deserve their own section. Helium-filled balloons, if let go, rise in the air until they begin to deflate at which point they fall back to Earth, most likely into the sea. Once in the sea they are an instant problem, particularly to marine mammals and turtles, which mistake them for jellyfish and can ingest them. The ribbons often found on balloons also pose the threat of entanglement to other animals such as seabirds. It is an easy mistake for a turtle to make, jellyfish being the favourite food of some species. Indeed Leatherback Turtles, the world's largest, travel all the way across the Atlantic Ocean from their breeding grounds in the Caribbean Sea to feast on jellyfish off our shores in the north-east Atlantic. Bearing in mind that Leatherback Turtles have been around for more than 100 million years, it is not surprising that they cannot distinguish between a jellyfish and a balloon in the sea.

Broadly speaking, there are three types of balloon commonly found on beach strandlines – latex balloons, foil balloons and weather balloons, and all have the potential to kill a marine animal. They enter the environment for different reasons, either as part of a celebratory balloon release or a fund-raising balloon race, individually as children accidentally let them go or, in the case of weather balloons, deliberately to help with weather forecasting.

Traditionally balloons have been used for celebrating special events such as weddings and birthdays, but they are increasingly being used for advertising and the balloons found on beaches often still have the company name emblazoned across them.

The problem of balloons in the environment is well recognised and many councils have now banned balloon releases from taking part on their land. Some organisations are finding alternative ways to celebrate or advertise themselves but the release of balloons, which some see as littering, is still a big environmental problem.

Toys

An endless variety of toys can be found on strandlines but some have been given a special importance as dedicated beachcombers seek them out to add to their collections. Some have been lost in great numbers from shipping containers, while others are most likely lost by children visiting the beach.

'Beach hero' is the generic name given to toy soldiers and super-heroes found on the beach. Some are given out free from fast-food outlets in children's meal boxes while others may be favourite toys regrettably lost.

When a container of plastic Kinder eggs was lost from the MSC *Napoli* the toy parts washed onto beaches in great numbers. Some people began collecting the parts and assembling the toys as a memento of the event, proof that there is fun to be had whilst removing plastic litter from the environment!

Retro rubbish

This term is given to items such as toys, crisp bags and drink bottles recognised by their design as being several decades old. Their existence is as an indication of how long plastic litter persists in the marine or beach environment, long after its useful life has ended. Glass and vulcanite bottle stoppers, dating from pre-plastic times, can sometimes be found, especially on town and harbour-side beaches, and may be stamped with the brewery's name. It is not always clear if the litter has been uncovered after being buried in the beach as sand has piled up on top, or whether it has been floating in the ocean gyre and eventually broken away and been carried inshore. Our nostalgia for earlier times makes these rare finds interesting and exciting, although at the same time they offer a warning about our plastic legacy.

Shotgun cartridges

One of the commonest items found on beaches all around the country are the plastic remains of empty 12 gauge shotgun cartridges. These are found in two parts – the coloured plastic shell and the colourless wads, the metal caps having corroded. There are a number of ways these can end up on beaches, including wildfowling both locally and abroad, and clay-pigeon shooting onboard cruise liners. Some may date from previous decades, when these activities were more commonplace.

Single-use plastic

This term describes everyday objects, such as plastic packaging, cotton buds, cups, bottles, drinking straws and carrier bags, which are used once and then discarded. Although some of them may be recycled into new products, they are intended to have a very short usable life, despite being made of a material designed to last. All kinds of single-use plastic items end up on beaches where some, such as bottles and bottle-tops, often make up the bulk of the litter found, while others are particularly harmful to marine wildlife. Plastic carrier bags, for example, are regularly found in the stomachs of turtles, whales and other marine animals, having been mistaken for jellyfish and ingested.

Sewage-related debris

Cotton bud sticks

The multi-coloured, plastic stems of cotton bud sticks can be found on beaches in huge numbers but are easily overlooked. They have several notches at either end where the cotton wool was attached, this distinguishes them from lolly sticks. They get into the sea and onto strandlines via the sewage system after being flushed down toilets.

WET WIPES – TO FLUSH OR NOT TO FLUSH?

Over recent years there has been a huge increase in the use of flushable but non-biodegradable products. Examples include wet wipe toilet tissues, disposable wipe and flush toilet cleaning cloths, make-up wipes and baby wipes, all of which contain plastic fibres. While these products may be desirable and convenient, they are causing an increasing problem to both water companies and beach users. As they do not break down in the sewage system they often cause blockages and must be removed at great cost. In the event of a CSO being opened in heavy rainfall they inevitably end up in the sea and in due course decorate strandlines in the most undesirable way.

The toilet should never be used as a bin and non-biodegradable products should not be flushed. Flushed items should always be restricted to toilet paper and the products of our own bodies!

This immense solid sewer blockage was formed from fat, wet wipes and other litter wrongly put down drains and toilets

Strandline
wildlife

A diverse and dynamic habitat

The beach strandline is just as much a wildlife habitat as a woodland or wildflower meadow, and every bit as diverse and interesting. It has a dynamic nature, changing every day as organic debris from the sea is deposited on the beach to be gradually broken down by the strandline inhabitants; sometimes the whole strandline is buried in sand or shingle or submerged by storm waves.

Some animals spend their whole lives in the strandline while others make use of it at certain times, taking advantage of the bounty it offers. An established and healthy strandline can support a huge abundance of organisms, and may be one of the richest terrestrial habitats we have. The sheer volume of animal life can be overwhelming and can be easily experienced by lifting a rock or piece of debris to find a mass of Sand Hoppers beneath, or visiting on a sunny day as swarms of seaweed flies emerge from the piles of seaweed.

Photographing birds on the strandline; complete camouflage isn't always necessary when photographing wildlife, but make sure your clothes are dull-coloured and as quiet as possible if you want to stay undetected

The strandline as a lifeline

Having a high salt content and being so close to the sea, the strandline rarely freezes. In fact it may generate its own heat as piles of seaweed can act like a giant compost heap, with the internal temperature up to 20°C higher than the air temperature. This offers ideal conditions for invertebrates to live year round, even in the depths of winter when most flying insects are either immature or hibernating and in turn, this unseasonal bounty can offer a lifeline to birds and mammals.

A harsh environment

The strandline is undoubtedly one of the harshest environments for animals to live. There is the regular threat of being washed away or buried in sand or shingle by storm waves, being submerged in salt water or dessicated by strong, salt-laden winds. Prolonged calm conditions may result in a lack of fresh material washing in and the availability of fresh water can be severely limited.

The strandline food web

Bacteria coating the surface of the seaweed and other organic debris starts the process of decomposition, just as happens to leaflitter on a woodland floor. This provides an abundant source of food for small invertebrates such as Sand Hoppers and seaweed flies, and mites which are almost too small for the naked eye to see. These are preyed upon by beetles, centipedes and spiders and so on up the food chain to birds, small rodents and bats.

At high tide marine invertebrates continue the recycling process, adding vital nutrients to the intertidal and shallow water marine ecosystem and providing abundant food for fish such as mullet and bass.

The decomposed organic material becomes incorporated into beach sediments and enables hardy pioneer beach plants such as oraches, Sea Rocket and Sea Sandwort to colonise and in turn collect more beach material such as wind-blown sand and organic debris. Eventually a succession of plants may colonise, attracting a whole new community of wildlife.

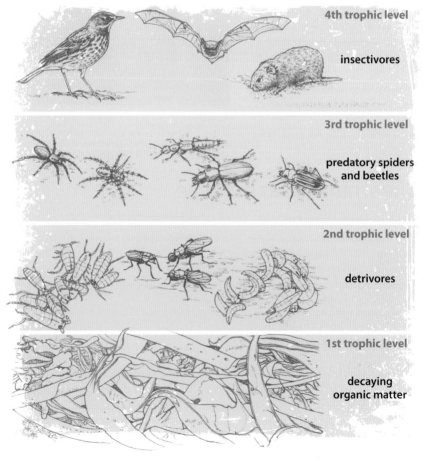

4th trophic level

insectivores

3rd trophic level

predatory spiders and beetles

2nd trophic level

detrivores

1st trophic level

decaying organic matter

Under-recorded and under-studied

The plants and animals that live on the strandline are largely under-recorded and not often described in seashore or other wildlife books. Because the strandline is partly a terrestrial and partly a marine habitat, it is widely overlooked by naturalists. Terrestrial ecologists tend to stop when they reach the back of the beach while marine ecologists step over the strandline to get to the sea and rockpools.

A simple survey we carried out on our local beaches uncovered new records of species on almost every visit. We hope that this book will encourage more people to take a closer look at strandline wildlife, and learn to love and value it. While some of the species living in strandlines can be found in other habitats, the majority are endemic to this environment, having evolved to survive in their harsh surroundings.

How to observe strandline wildlife

Strandlines are easily accessible and great places to discover and observe wildlife. Although few people will appreciate a swarm of seaweed flies, these indicate a healthy strandline and attract other, more welcome wildlife, such as birds and bats, for the observer to enjoy.

Birdwatching While some birds live permanently on the beach, many use the strandline to feed up during migration, either as they arrive in spring or before they depart in autumn. The best time of day is early morning before the beach is busy with dog walkers and other visitors. By using binoculars to observe the birds that are present on the strandline, watchers should be able to see how they are using it; rummaging in the seaweed or snatching flying insects out of the air. Adopting simple field-craft such as being quiet, patient and wearing natural-coloured or camouflaged clothing will enable closer encounters and enhance your experience.

Pied Wagtail, *Motacilla alba*, catching seaweed flies

Night time beach safari A twilight excursion to the beach can be an exciting and rewarding adventure. A calm, moonlit night is best but check for low tide before venturing out. Once you have found a safe place to settle, turn off your torch and allow your eyes to adjust to the dark. Bats can sometimes be observed swooping over the beach and water and may be seen without the aid of a bat detector, although one of these gadgets would help you identify the species and would also alert you to their presence. A bright lantern placed and left on the beach may attract a multitude of Sand Hoppers to it, clambering over each other to reach the light (see opposite). Small and large mammals, including Foxes, voles and Hedgehogs, often visit the strandline in search of food and can be encountered on a night-time safari. Look for footprints in the sand and shine your torch along the beach every now and again. The quieter you are the more likely you are to see any mammals.

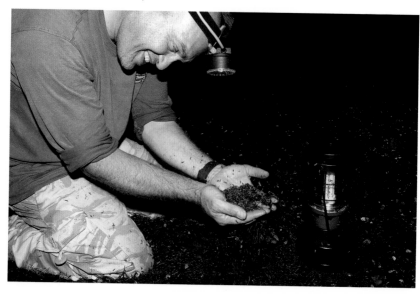

SAND HOPPER NIGHT SAFARI

Under cover of darkness, a good way to witness the extraordinary abundance of sand and beach hoppers on a strandline is to place a deep tray or washing-up bowl into the strandline so the top is level with the surrounding material. Put a battery-powered lantern into the tray and leave. Before long you should see the hoppers emerging and moving towards the light. In some instances, the sheer abundance of animals collecting around the light can be astonishing.

NB: Use of a gas or fuel-powered light is not recommended for this activity as the heat produced will kill them.

Threats to strandline wildlife

In recent decades, plastic litter has become a major component in beach strandlines with the result that many tourist beaches are now cleaned mechanically. This is done by driving a tractor along the beach, towing a rake which removes the top 20cm of sand, filtering out the larger items and replacing the sand and smaller items (such as cigarette butts and bottle tops). The organic debris is removed along with the litter and the sand is compacted by the vehicle, destroying the habitat. In some instances the reason for cleaning is purely to remove the seaweed or seagrass and prevent its decomposition on the beach, which is perceived as a health hazard for visitors, contrary to recommendations by seaside tourism award schemes. Unfortunately the removal of strandline material inevitably prevents stabilisation of the substrate and impedes the development of sand dunes which act as a natural coastal defence.

Pollutants released into the sea, accidentally or deliberately, can inevitably wash onto strandlines. In recent years examples of palm oil, Polyisobutene (PIB) and oil spills have all affected strandline wildlife in the UK. They cause a

Rancid vegetable oil

Tar balls with embedded nurdles and other plastic fragments

Paraffin wax

potential hazard for anything that encounters them, large or small, including humans and dogs.

Microplastics are microscopic granules of plastic, either manufactured for use in cosmetic and cleaning products or formed as a result of plastic marine litter breaking into smaller pieces. It is well-documented that microplastics are abundant in the world's oceans and are ingested by marine life. They may also be incorporated in strandline material, where they accumulate and are potentially eaten by wildlife.

Coastal squeeze is the term used when beaches become trapped between rising sea levels and hard coastal defences (see page 13). Under natural conditions coastal habitats retreat landward in the face of advancing sea levels but when sea walls and other infrastructure are placed at the back of the beach their retreat is prevented, and eventually the wildlife habitat is squeezed out of existence. In many places where a strandline would once have existed the waves now reach the back of the beach, leaving no room for the habitat to develop.

Microplastics removed from just one tube of facial scrub

Work to restore a shingle bank defence

Strandline wildlife conservation

The conservation of strandlines and their associated wildlife is important both for people and nature. Many of the species found on strandlines are endemic – found nowhere else. Due to a decline in the occurrence and health of this habitat some are also very rare. Allowing a strandline to develop and be colonised by pioneer plants can help stabilise the substrate and slow down erosion. It might even begin the process of sand dune formation, an effective natural coastal defence.

Hand-picking litter from beaches is environmentally preferable to mechanical cleaning and can also be less costly. It is more selective, only removing the non-organic debris, and is less damaging to the structure of the beach. Ultimately the problem of marine litter must be tackled at source to prevent it entering the sea. We can all play our part by ensuring our litter is disposed of responsibly and that we do not use the toilet as a rubbish bin. The need to reduce our plastic consumption on a worldwide scale is urgent and we should start by ending our reliance on single-use plastic and over-packaging of products. In the face of inactivity by governments and corporations, it is down to us as consumers to take action.

Microplastics, labeled polyethylene (PE) or polypropylene (PP) on the ingredients list, are now used in many cosmetic products and toothpastes. They have substituted natural resources such as salt, coconut and plant seeds that were previously used for cleaning or exfoliating, and are designed to be washed away down drains after use, passing easily through filters and ending up in the sea.

There is a growing movement towards finding alternatives to single-use plastic. As consumers, we have the choice to be part of the solution or part of the problem. Saying 'no' to plastic carrier bags, drinking straws, bottled water and products containing microplastics, sends a clear message to retailers. There is a wealth of information and advice available online to help find natural alternatives and break the plastic habit.

The coastline is a dynamic and ever-changing place, with some parts eroding and others expanding as new material is deposited by the sea. In many places around our coastline, sea defences have been built to hold back the sea and protect property. However, with climate change causing sea levels to rise faster now than in the past, and with more severe-weather events happening, we need to understand that we cannot always prevent coastal change. New solutions to the problem include embracing and adapting to these natural changes and, where possible, allowing the coastline to evolve under managed conditions, taking advantage of the benefits it may present. For the future of coastal habitats, including strandlines, this is a much better strategy than building hard sea defences.

Invertebrates

Sand and Beach Hoppers

A number of species from this group have been recorded in the UK, although only two are common. They belong to the group of crustaceans called amphipods, which are distinguished by their laterally flattened body shape with a curved back and flea-like appearance. Most amphipods live in the sea, whereas Sand and Beach Hoppers are terrestrial animals and cannot survive underwater. Their hopping action is produced by tucking their tail (telson) underneath the body and rapidly flicking it out. They can sometimes be seen retreating up the beach as the tide comes in.

Sand Hopper *Talitrus saltator*

Below: burrowing Sand Hopper

Size 20mm

Sand Hoppers are found on sandy beaches where they live in burrows at depths of up to 30cm (inset opposite), emerging at night to feed on detritus on the strandline. They are pale grey in colour, with white eyes and one antenna longer and thicker than the other. When disturbed, for example by turning over strandline seaweed, they tend to hop frantically to escape both predation and the light, and will quickly burrow beneath the sand.

The Sand Hoppers' pencil-sized holes can easily be seen around strandline debris (inset below). When the tide comes in, a Sand Hopper will enter its burrow and back-fill the tunnel behind it to plug it against entry by seawater. Small wading birds, such as Dunlin and Sanderling, look for the depressions in the sand which mark the burrows, inserting their bills to pick the animals out from below.

Below: Sand Hopper burrows

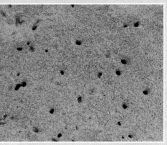

Beach Hopper *Orchestia gammarellus*

Size 18mm

This amphipod is similar in shape to the Sand Hopper. It can range in colour from a reddish-brown to grey and has a dark eye. This animal is found on rocky beaches with a limited supply of sand and so it does not burrow but lives beneath rocks and debris around the high water mark. It lies on its side but hops to find new cover if disturbed. It can be uncovered in surprising abundance when large items are turned over and it is important to restore items to their original position to ensure their survival.

SETTING A PITFALL TRAP

A pitfall trap is a small pot buried into the beach substrate amongst the strandline material and shielded with a lid that doesn't close it off. The lid must keep rain water out but allow small invertebrates to fall into the pot. Try plastic slug traps, which can be cheaply bought from garden centres or hardware stores. Your pot should be set in the evening and covered with seaweed, driftwood and other beach material, and marked in some way so you can find it again in the morning. To avoid the trap filling with sea water at high tide, you must set it above the high tide mark on that day, but within the strandline itself. This is best done in the warmer months so that your catch survives the night in the trap, and during calm conditions to avoid a stray wave filling it.

Step 1
Bait the trap – for example with cat biscuits. This is optional but the smell of the food may attract invertebrates.

Step 2
Scrape or dig a depression in the strandline and position your pot in it with the lid at beach surface level. Place a marker beside your pot so you can find it again, and then cover it in seaweed or litter to hide it.

Step 3
Return early the next morning with a pale-coloured tray or bowl and empty the pot contents into it for examination. A magnifier may be useful to aid identification. Release the animals when finished.

Seaweed flies

Seaweed fly, sometimes referred to as kelp or wrack fly, is a generic term for flies associated with seaweed on the strandline. There are several other types of shore fly, not associated with the strandline, which are not mentioned here. They are one of the most noticeable species on the strandline when on warm days swarms emerge from the seaweed, proving a nuisance to beach visitors. Flies are usually associated with an unhygienic environment and are not generally appreciated by humans. However, seaweed flies pose no threat to us; they are one of the key components of this wildlife habitat and are found nowhere else.

The whole life-cycle of a seaweed fly is completed in the beach strandline. The breeding adults are attracted to fresh seaweed deposits, in which they lay their eggs. The maggots, which are able to survive the high salt content, emerge and feed on bacteria coating the seaweed, before forming pupae. The empty, black, oval pupal cases can sometimes be found in large numbers among small items of debris at the back of the strandline. The live ones develop underneath heavy objects such as rocks and driftwood where they are less likely to be disturbed by waves and predators. On warm days the new adult flies emerge *en masse* to start the process again.

Above: seaweed fly maggot
Right: seaweed fly pupae

Coelopidae

These are the most commonly encountered seaweed flies in the UK. Two of the species are common and can be seen together. As the tide comes in they move up the shore and at high water they collect pollen from flowers, unlike other shore flies. These are medium-sized flies with a distinctive flat body, often seen walking as opposed to flying, even when disturbed.

Coelopa frigida is sometimes referred to as the Bristly-legged Seaweed Fly, the bristles on its pale legs being the main identifying feature.

Coelopa pilipes has distinctly hairy, almost furry-looking, dark-coloured legs.

Malacomyia sciomyzina is another coelopid found on strandlines. It is pale in colour with a yellowish abdomen.

USING A POOTER

A pooter is a small pot used to catch live insects for closer examination and identification, without having to handle them. It consists of a clear pot with a lid into which two tubes are inserted. The idea is to suck through one tube while holding the end of the other above a small fly or beetle. The air sucked out of the pot results in air being sucked in through the second tube, along with the target invertebrate. A fine mesh over the internal end of the sucking tube prevents you from inhaling the bugs. Once you have collected your strandline minibeasts they can either be examined in situ or carefully transferred to a magnifying pot. Release all animals when finished.

Pooters and magnifiers are inexpensive and available online from ecological equipment suppliers.

Orygma luctuosum

This species is a member of the Sepsidae family. It is a relatively common seaweed fly, usually found with the Coelopidae species on the seaweed of the strandline. However, it can be found in a wide range of strandlines, including sparse and sandy shore strandlines. It does not tend to swarm in huge numbers like the Coelopidae flies.

Thoracochaeta zosterae

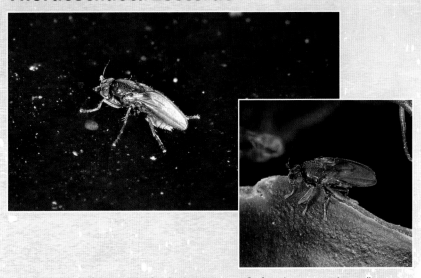

A member of the Sphaeroceridae family, this is a minute fly, found on seaweed strandlines. It can be very common but is impossible to identify with any certainty in the field.

Helcomyza ustulata

A member of the Heleomyzidae family, this is a large fly, found on sandy-shore strandlines. It is a predatory fly with a very distinctive behaviour – zig-zagging along a metre or so at a time between hiding places. This behaviour is obvious as you walk along a sandy beach strandline. The fly is pale with long wings that completely cover its abdomen when closed.

Hecamede albicans

This minute fly has a distinctive metallic green body and opaque white wings. It is found on decaying animals on the strandline, and also seaweed.

Anthomyiidae

This family contains three common strandline species which are associated with dead animals rather than seaweed. They are small, greyish flies, similar in appearance to the more familiar house-fly. The place to look for these is around stranded goose barnacles, dead fish and crabs on all types of beaches. The three species, which cannot be identified from one another in the field, are **Fucellia maritima**, **Fucellia tergina** and **Fucellia fucorum**.

Fucellia maritima

Above and below: *Fucellia tergina*

FLY COCOONS

A very rare find is the egg-shaped cocoon of a coastal fly, *Machaerium maritimae*, which is built from sand grains. A number of these were found washing up onto a beach in south Wales with the developing pupae still inside, while others had already been vacated and had an exit hole at one end. Each cocoon measured around 10mm long.

Isopods (woodlouse-like animals)

Sea Slater *Ligia oceanica*

Size 30mm

A very common, large, fast-moving isopod of rocky seashores found in crevices, under rocks and driftwood and amongst strandline debris. It is nocturnal, feeding on decaying seaweed and is grey to olive green in colour. The best time to see these animals in action is at night with a torch.

Halophiloscia couchii

Size 10mm

A rare, pinkish-brown isopod which is distinguished by its long antennae. It is found at the back of the beach on boulder and shingle beaches or those with rocky cliffs. It is most easily found by lifting rocks at the back of the beach.

Armadillidium album

Size 6mm

A rare isopod of sandy beaches, where it lives under driftwood and strandline debris. It is sandy-coloured and partly rolls up when disturbed, leaving a few legs protruding to cling onto the substrate. It is associated with undisturbed sand-dune systems and likes a particular size of sand grain. It can be found beneath strandline debris, where it clings to the underside of driftwood or burrows deep in the sand.

Common Rough Woodlouse *Porcellio scaber*

Size 17mm

This is the familiar woodlouse of homes and gardens. It is very common and widespread, not restricted to beaches. The colour is mostly a uniform slate-grey but orange, cream and mottled varieties are frequently found, especially by the coast. If found under rocks and strandline debris it will remain motionless, unlike other strandline isopods which tend to run away.

Common Shiny Woodlouse *Oniscus asellus*

Size 17mm

A very common woodlouse with a shiny, flattened body and pale dots along the edges. The colour is usually grey with irregular pale markings and yellow patches but yellow and orange varieties can be found by the coast. It is often found with the Common Rough Woodlouse and their behaviour is similar.

Centipedes

Strigamia maritima

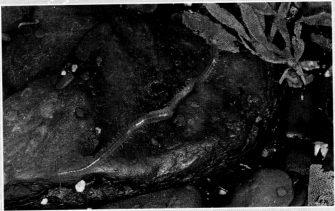

Size 120mm

An exclusively coastal centipede found under rocks and strandline debris. It preys on small invertebrates and also scavenges dead animal matter. It has a pair of claws which inject venom to subdue its prey. Nests, sometimes with juveniles inside, can be found under large pieces of driftwood and litter.

Ground beetles – Carabidae

These are beetles whose wing cases (elytra) cover their abdomen.

Beachcomber Beetle *Eurynebria complanata*

Size 15mm

This rare ground beetle is perfectly evolved to live on the strandline of sandy beaches. Its elytra are sandy-coloured with black markings and it can be found underneath large pieces of driftwood. It is a fast-moving predator of Sand Hoppers and other small invertebrates. This species is restricted to sandy beaches backed by undisturbed sand-dune systems.

Broscus cephalotes

Size 23mm
A large, black beetle not restricted to, but most often found on sandy beaches backed by sand dunes, living beneath large pieces of driftwood and litter where it is undisturbed. It is a predator of Sand Hoppers and isopods above the high tide mark and when found may remain motionless. It is most active at night when it can be seen in the open.

Darkling Beetle *Phaleria cadaverina*

Size 8mm

A small, widespread beetle of sandy beaches found on dead animals, particularly seabirds and under strandline material. It is sandy-coloured with black markings and when handled it plays dead. This beetle is most easily found among the feathers of dead seabirds on the strandline.

Paranchus albipes

Size 9mm

This small, black beetle with pale legs is associated with freshwater. Although not restricted to the coast it can be very common on the strandline on all types of beach where there is freshwater in streams or run-off from cliffs. It is fast-moving when disturbed, preys on small invertebrates and can be found in high numbers under stones and debris.

Shore Sexton Beetle *Necrodes littoralis*

Size 23mm

A large, black beetle with ridged wing cases, which burrows into large carcasses. It can be found under strandline debris, especially on animal corpses, but is also regularly found in moth traps. Reportedly it gives off a pungent odour when disturbed.

Cercyon spp.

Size 2–4mm

A number of species belonging to this genus can be found under strandline algae and on driftwood. They are tiny, oval beetles with club-shaped antennae. They can be common but being tiny are easily overlooked. They cannot be identified to species in the field.

Rove beetles – Staphylinidae

These are beetles whose elytra or wing cases do not completely cover their long, flexible abdomens.

Cafius xantholoma

Size 9mm
This beetle can be abundant on rocky shore strandlines and may swarm in the daytime, the flying adults often being mistaken for seaweed flies. It is a predator of Sand Hoppers and other small invertebrates and can be found under strandline items or active in amongst seaweed, both by day and night. The prefix 'xantho' (meaning yellow) refers to the row of tiny yellow hairs along its sides which are visible with a hand lens and distinguish it from other, similar species.

Aleochara obscurella

Size 4.5mm
A small, black rove beetle found on rocky shore strandlines amongst debris, where it preys on small invertebrates. It lacks the yellow hairs of *Cafius xantholoma* but is otherwise similar, which may account for why it is rarely recorded.

Omalium laeviusculum

Size 4mm

A very small, reddish-brown rove beetle with a short, stout abdomen measuring double the length of the wing cases. It can be seen swarming in the daytime on stony or shingle beaches. Otherwise it is found under driftwood and other strandline debris.

Hairy Rove Beetle *Creophilus maxillosus*

Size 12–23mm

This beetle is not restricted to strandlines, but when it is, it is found on animal carcasses, mainly birds, where it hunts small invertebrates that are feeding on the carrion. Hairs on the abdomen give it a slightly hairy appearance when viewed through a hand lens. It produces a chemical mixture from a gland in its abdomen to deter predators.

Paederus littoralis

Size 9mm
A colourful rove beetle with bold red and black banding, this species can be active in daylight. It is a predator, and although not restricted to the coast, is found beneath strandline debris and stones as well as on cliffs and open coasts.

Bledius spectabilis

Size 7mm
A black rove beetle with red elytra which look like a red waistcoat. It burrows in the soft banks of lagoons and saltmarshes, leaving visible mounds of excavated material (inset). Although it is not found on the open coast it is something to look out for under strandlines in these specialist habitats.

Crickets, earwigs and springtails

Scaly Cricket *Pseudomogoplistes vicentae*

Size 13mm

An internationally rare, wingless cricket, so far recorded at only a handful of sites in the British Isles. It has a chestnut brown to grey body with pale legs which are covered in tiny scales. It is endemic to shingle beach strandlines, where it can be found under stones and amongst pebbles and strandline material, emerging at night to feed on dead animal and plant matter.

Common Earwig *Forficula auricularia*

Size 13mm

The Common Earwig is found in many habitats and is a familiar animal of gardens. It is also frequently seen on strandlines where it feeds on small invertebrates, detritus and plant material. It is reddish-brown in colour with a flattened, elongated abdomen ending in a pair of 'pincers'.

Springtails Collembola

Size 2–4mm

Springtails make up a large group containing some of the smallest and possibly the most abundant insects on Earth. They are found in a great variety of habitats, including the strandline where they live under debris. They are wingless and get their English name from their mode of locomotion whereby a special hooked appendage, tucked beneath their abdomen, is used to give them leverage to jump. Identification to species level is not possible in the field.

Strandline spiders and mites

Strandline spiders are predatory animals, catching and feeding on other invertebrates. Although a wide variety of spiders are associated with coastal habitats such as vegetated shingle and sand dunes, only a limited number are found amongst strandline debris. As these spiders are very specialised to the strandline habitat they tend to be rare.

Mites belong to the same group as spiders, the Arachnida, and are a large group found in a great variety of habitats, including as parasites on animals. On the strandline they parasitise strandline invertebrates such as beetles and seaweed flies and there are also some larger, free-living species which are visible to the naked eye. The mites in this section are identifiable in the field and can look spectacular under a hand lens.

A wolf spider hunting on a shingle beach

Halorates reprobus

Body length 3mm
Halorates reprobus is a type of money spider restricted to coastal habitats, in particular the beach strandline. This tiny spider is reddish-brown in colour and can be found nesting in depressions in driftwood and in empty shells where it builds a silk cocoon. The few European records for this species indicate that UK populations may be of international importance.

French Zipper Spider *Drassyllus lutetianus*

Body length 5–7.5mm
This medium-sized black, shiny spider can be found amongst wet strandline debris, especially on shingle beaches.

Wolf spiders Lycosidae

Body length 4–9mm

Wolf spiders are covered in fine hairs and tend to be found in shingle or under strandline debris where they can be abundant in pitfall traps. They are active hunters, both by day and night. Wolf spiders do not build a web but are fast runners, chasing down their prey.

Sand Wolf Spider *Arctosa perita*

Body length 5–9mm

A spider of sandy beaches with excellent camouflage and therefore difficult to spot unless it moves. It is active during the day and can be found amongst strandline debris and in sand dunes.

Velvet mites Trombidiidae

Size 1–2mm

These tiny, spider-like animals are scarlet in colour, their bodies resembling a crumpled, velvet pin-cushion. They are carnivorous, feeding on small invertebrates in the strandline, although they are not restricted to the coast.

Red Snout Mite *Neomolgus littoralis*

Size 3.5mm

Although there are a number of red snout mites, *Neomolgus littoralis* is the most likely to be found on the strandline where it feeds on seaweed flies. It is a bright red mite with elongated mouthparts resembling a snout. It can also be found elsewhere on the seashore.

Other mites

Mites are an important group of strandline animals and are often common and abundant, although because of their size they tend to be overlooked. Although shapes differ, identification to species in the field is not possible. Examples of other mite groups are Halolaelapidae, Parastidae and Macrochelidae.

Halolaelapidae

Parastidae

Macrochelidae

Strandline birds

The strandline is a rich source of food for a wide variety of birds, providing an abundance of invertebrates, carrion in the form of dead animals washed ashore, and seeds from beach plants. Birds using the strandline range from those that live there almost full time to those that stop off to feed themselves up during their migration, or live in coastal habitats and gardens and use it on a regular basis; from large Ravens and Black-backed Gulls to tiny Wrens and Snow Buntings; from sea and shore birds to those more familiar in terrestrial habitats.

The strandline also offers a life-line to small birds during the colder, winter months, providing a source of food all year round when other food may be in short supply. A large marine mammal carcass may keep carrion birds supplied for many months.

Birds feeding on the strandline are often overlooked by beach visitors. The best time to spot them is early morning, before the beach walkers arrive to scare them away. A pair of binoculars and clothing in natural colours will allow a glimpse not only into which birds are present but also into their feeding and territorial behaviour and the types of food they are selecting. Understanding the needs and behaviours of these birds enables us to appreciate the importance of the piles of rotting seaweed and flying insects that are often regarded as a nuisance.

In theory, almost any bird could be seen on a beach at some time or other. The ones listed here are those that are known to regularly use strandline habitats, and the accounts detail why these birds are there and their behaviour. There are many bird books on the market for those who want to know more.

Rock Pipit feeding on seaweed flies

Seabirds

Black-headed Gull *Chroicocephalus ridibundus*

Size 38cm

A small gull with a chocolate brown hood during the breeding season, although it loses this in winter and has a white head with dark smudges above and behind the eye. It has red legs and a reddish bill (darker in summer). It is usually seen in flocks and is very vocal. This bird often flocks on the beach and on close inspection can be seen to be picking flying strandline insects from the air. It also rafts on water in the shallows as the tide comes in, picking seaweed flies and maggots from the surface of the water where they have been flushed from the strandline.

Herring Gull *Larus argentatus*

Size 62cm

This is the most familiar of our gulls and its mewing call is iconic of British holidays and seaside towns. Adults sport a snowy white head and body with silver grey wings, a sturdy, bright, yellow bill with a red spot, and pink legs. It is an opportunistic species and is widely persecuted for making use of the waste we leave behind. Unfortunately this gull has undergone a long and severe decline and now has Red List conservation status. Groups of Herring Gulls forage along strandlines looking for washed up molluscs, crabs and other carrion.

Great Black-backed Gull *Larus marinus*

Size 78cm

This is the world's largest gull. It has a large yellow bill, pinkish legs and dark grey to black wings. It dwarfs other gulls on the strandline where it scavenges for carrion such as bird and mammal carcasses and food waste left by people. It will also take live animals such as voles and the chicks of beach-nesting birds.

Shorebirds

Rock Pipit *Anthus petrosus*

Size 17cm

A brown-backed bird with a brown-speckled, yellowish breast and brown legs and bill. It is a true seashore bird, living on rocky beaches year-round, feeding on seashore molluscs at low tide, as well as insects and Sand Hoppers on the strandline. This is a vocal and territorial bird

which chases other birds off its patch. It will stand on prominent piles of seaweed where it can snatch flying insects from the air, or turns over seaweed debris taking maggots and other invertebrates.

Pied Wagtail *Motacilla alba*

Size 18cm

A black and white bird, which, like all wagtails, pumps its tail up and down. It has a black patch on the top of its head and breast and a white face and underside. It is not restricted to coastal habitats but is very common on sea shores where it feeds on small molluscs, insects and seeds. It may be seen squabbling over territory with Rock Pipits. Flying strandline insects are caught by jumping from prominent piles of seaweed, splaying the wings like a parachute.

Carrion Crow *Corvus corone*

Size 50cm

A solitary, large, black, glossy bird with a stout, black bill and legs. Very common on beaches, this bird can be seen rummaging through strandline material looking for carrion, molluscs and crabs on which it feeds. They will fly up holding a mollusc and drop it from a height aiming to break open the shell. Stacks of slipper limpets are a favourite where these are found.

Hooded Crow *Corvus cornix*

Size 50cm

This crow is a northern species that is closely related to the Carrion Crow and may interbreed with it where the two species overlap. It has a distinctive grey and black body and feeds on carrion on the strandline, often in groups. Unlike the Carrion Crow the Hooded Crow can be timid and unapproachable.

Jackdaw *Corvus monedula*

Size 34cm

A small crow with glossy black feathers, a grey nape and jet black cap, black legs and bill. It has a very pale blue eye. Jackdaws are often in small groups and are common on beaches at all times of year, where they tend to pick around in the strandline seaweed. They have a varied diet and will eat invertebrates and seeds as well as carrion.

Raven *Corvus corax*

Size 67cm

The world's largest crow, this all-black bird has a shaggy throat and thick-set bill, and makes a deep 'cronking' call. From a distance it could be mistaken for a carrion crow but is a much larger bird and the call is distinctive. The Raven is a bird of mountains, rocky crags and cliffs of western Britain and following years of decline the population appears to be increasing and spreading east. It is usually seen in pairs and is a carrion-feeder and predator of small mammals and birds, often flying along the strandline looking for a likely meal.

Oystercatcher *Haematopus ostralegus*

Size 45cm

An unmistakable black and white wading bird with a long, bright orange bill and a red eye. It is very common on all seashores and in estuaries, usually in flocks or small groups, where it feeds on molluscs either attached to rocks or buried in sand and mud. These birds patrol the strandline at high tide looking for washed up shellfish and have a distinctive alarm call when disturbed.

Ringed Plover *Charadrius hiaticula*

Size 19cm

A small, brown wader with a white belly, chin and forehead and a dark breast-band. It has a dumpy shape and a short bill. It can be seen on a variety of beaches, although it nests mainly on shingle beaches. It is hard to spot until it moves, running in short bursts along the water's edge, looking for insects and worms, or along the strandline at high tide.

Turnstone *Arenaria interpres*

Above: Turnstone, winter plumage

Left: Turnstone, summer plumage

Size 24cm

This bird overwinters in the UK but migrates to Canada and Greenland for breeding, although non-breeding birds can be seen here in the summer. They are well-camouflaged on the seashore amongst seaweed and are often only spotted when they move. Normally present in small groups, this is a wading bird that prefers picking among seaweed-covered rocks and is often found along harbour walls in towns, where it seems unperturbed by human presence. At high tide, Turnstones will turn over piles of strandline seaweed searching for Sand Hoppers and other small crustaceans.

Sanderling *Calidris alba*

Size 21cm

A small, pale wading bird of sandy beaches, where it runs along the water's edge searching for marine worms and crustaceans which it takes from burrows in the sand. The black legs and bill contrast with the pale grey and white body. It overwinters in the UK after breeding in the Arctic, although non-breeding birds can be seen all year round, usually in small groups. At high tide it will search for Sand Hoppers along the strandline.

Dunlin *Calidris alpina*

Dunlin, summer plumage

Size 20cm

A small, wading bird, with a russet, mottled back and pale underside, and a long, black bill which is slightly down-curved. It breeds in the UK but numbers are swelled in the winter when it can be seen in very large flocks, especially in estuaries. Dunlins often associate on beaches with Sanderlings, foraging at the water's edge and on the strandline at high tide.

Dunlin, winter plumage

Common Sandpiper *Actitis hypoleucos*

Size 21cm

This small wading bird breeds in Wales and further north during the summer months, but can be seen in the south during migration and in the winter. Although not restricted to the coast it can be seen feeding on invertebrates along the strandline. During the breeding season, its persistent piping call may draw attention to its presence as it stands on prominent rocks on the seashore.

Purple Sandpiper *Calidris maritima*

Size 22cm

A mostly brown bird with a white underside, yellow legs and yellow bill with a dark tip. Purple Sandpipers are found on rocky seashores where they feed on intertidal molluscs and on insects, spiders and other invertebrates among fresh strandline debris at the water's edge.

Chats and thrushes

Stonechat *Saxicola torquata*

Size 12cm

A small songbird associated with gorse thickets of coastal cliffs and heathland. Males have distinctive plumage with a black head and throat, white collar and russet breast; females have a paler throat and head. They are easily identified by their call which sounds like two stones clinking together. On suitable beaches, where there is gorse behind, this bird may take advantage of the strandline bounty, taking insects from the air or invertebrates and seeds from the ground.

Robin *Erithacus rubecula*

Size 14cm

A very familiar bird of gardens with a brown back and red breast. By the coast, Robins may take advantage of the supply of strandline insects, invertebrates and seeds, especially during the winter months. Although not commonly seen on beaches, this species illustrates the way our more familiar terrestrial birds will forage on the beach when times are hard inland.

Wheatear *Oenanthe oenanthe*

Size 15cm

Males sport a blue-grey back (females a pale, sandy-grey back) and both sexes have a white rump and underparts and a buff throat and breast. The Wheatear breeds quite widely in the UK and migrates to Africa to overwinter. During migration, either on arrival in March or when departing in October, Wheatears are frequently seen on beaches as they stop off to feed up on insects and crustaceans.

Wren *Troglodytes troglodytes*

Size 10cm

A familiar, tiny, brown bird of gardens and scrub, with a distinctive upright tail. Coastal Wrens may nest in cliffs and scrub at the back of the beach and make frequent use of the strandline as a food source. They tend to remain hidden, quickly darting out when they spot an item of food such as an insect or spider, before retreating back under cover.

Snow Bunting *Plectrophenax nivalis*

Size 17cm

A winter visitor from its arctic breeding grounds, this small, dumpy bird has a mottled brown back and pale underside, with a short, triangular, yellow bill. A few pairs breed in north Scotland. During the winter it inhabits coastal areas, particularly favouring shingle beaches, where it feeds on strandline seeds and invertebrates. Amongst shingle it is very well camouflaged and hard to spot unless it moves.

Swifts, swallows and martins

Swallow, *Hirundo rustica*

These summer visitors breed in the UK before migrating to Africa for the winter. In late summer they often congregate on coasts actively feeding on seaweed flies, swooping low over the strandline and shallows in preparation for their long migration.

Mammals and amphibians

A variety of mammals and two species of toad are known to forage on strandline material. They may visit opportunistically, as is the case for larger mammals such as Foxes and Badgers which may smell a stranded carcass or dead seabird; or they may inhabit heath, scrub or soft cliffs at the back of the beach and visit on a nightly basis to feed on the invertebrates and vegetation that lives there. Although rarely seen during the day they often leave clues such as tracks and droppings. On a night-time beach safari you may be lucky to catch one in torch-light. This section lists some of the smaller species that visit the strandline on a regular basis.

Rodents and shrews

Wood Mouse, *Apodemus sylvaticus*

Brown Rat, *Rattus norvegicus*

Voles, mice, rats and shrews are all recorded actively foraging amongst strandline material, taking a wide variety of food from insects and their larvae to carrion and plant seeds. In adverse weather conditions, the strandline supplies a lifeline to the smaller mammals when other food sources are limited. These animals can sometimes be seen both during daylight and at night, without having to do a scientific trapping survey. A bit of patience and simple field craft may offer you a glimpse – turning over larger strandline items can disturb resting small mammals so take care to replace each item to its original position.

Field Vole, *Microtus agrestis*

Pygmy Shrew, *Sorex minutus*

Hedgehog *Erinaceus europaeus*

Size 25cm

The link between Hedgehogs and strandlines is under-studied but their footprints have been found on sandy beaches around the strandline. It is possible that they visit opportunistically to feed on invertebrates, carrion or mice.

Bats

Greater Horseshoe Bat, *Rhinolophus ferrumequinum*

Although little research has been done on the importance of strandlines for bats they can sometimes be recorded in high numbers at dusk, swooping low to collect flying insects. Common and Soprano Pipistrelles have both been recorded in good numbers but it is possible that other species take advantage of the abundance of these insects in summer and autumn. A bat detector will help alert you to their presence and will identify the species but moonlight is all that is needed to see these animals. Bats may visit strandlines on an opportunistic basis from nearby roosts in woodlands, buildings or sea caves.

Toads

At first glance, sandy beaches do not seem to be the ideal place to see amphibians, however the Natterjack Toad is a true coastal species and the Common Toad can sometimes be found beneath strandline debris where there are freshwater pools nearby.

Common Toad *Bufo bufo*

Size Up to 13cm
The Common Toad is brown in colour with a warty appearance. It is found in a wide variety of habitats and does not need to live near water except during the breeding season.

Natterjack Toad *Epidalea calamita*

Size Up to 8cm
The Natterjack Toad is distinguished from the Common Toad by the thin, yellow stripe down its back. It is very vocal during the breeding season (April to July) when, at night, the males serenade the females from the edge of their shallow breeding pools, competing to be the

Mating Natterjack Toads

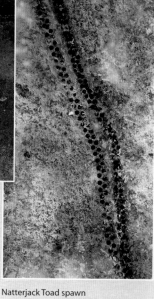

Natterjack Toad spawn

loudest and therefore most desirable. It is reported that their chorus can be heard from several kilometres away.

After breeding the females lay single strings of eggs (spawn) in the ponds which hatch into small, black tadpoles, gradually developing into toadlets, already exhibiting the characteristic yellow stripe. The toadlets leave the pools and live in sandy burrows with a D-shaped entrance, often living together. Natterjacks hibernate in their burrows in winter.

Natterjack Toads are rare in Britain, known almost exclusively from coastal locations where they are mainly associated with sand-dune systems, heaths and grazing marshes. They require shallow pools as they can drown in deep water and a minimum temperature is needed for successful breeding. The ideal pools are often found in sand dune slacks.

After dark, these toads can be observed on strandlines adjacent to their breeding pools and burrows where they feed on strandline invertebrates such as beetles and spiders. They also use strandline material to shelter from predators such as Hedgehogs, herons and gulls.

WARNING: Natterjack Toads are strictly protected by British and European law and care must be taken not to disturb them or damage their habitat.

Juvenile Natterjack Toads peering out of their protective sandy burrow

Strandline plants

Only a handful of plants actually grow on the strandline. They are the pioneering species that help create the right conditions for a succession of plants to grow on beaches that are accumulating material. In fact they help to put that process in place.

Organic strandline material breaks down and is buried in sand and shingle where it forms pockets packed with nutrients and rainwater, which it soaks up like a sponge. Pioneering strandline plants tap into this, and because they have evolved to survive the harsh conditions of a beach – the strong winds, salty atmosphere, mobile substrate and occasional inundation by waves – they can survive just above the high tide line. Once established they are able to trap wind-blown sand or wave-thrown pebbles and other strandline debris, and also produce their own organic matter in the form of dead leaves and stems. As the sand or shingle builds up at their seaward edge the strandline moves forward and the pioneer plants are replaced by less hardy beach species which outcompete them for space and nutrients. They in turn are now able to colonise forward of their first position. In this way sand dunes and shingle ridges develop in a series of lines, advancing towards the sea.

Prickly Saltwort helping to develop a fore dune

Specialist seashore plants usually have particular adaptations to enable them to live in the harsh environment of a beach, where they are subject to the drying effects of salt and wind and there is a limited supply of freshwater and nutrients. They often share similar features with desert vegetation. Fleshy, hairy and rolled leaves are designed to hold onto the limited amount of freshwater and reduce its evaporation from the leaf surface. Very long and extensive root systems help the plant to seek out pockets of organic material, often buried deep below. Seeds are sometimes designed to be transported by the sea, a good adaptation for a plant living in an unstable environment, ensuring that it can colonise new, more suitable areas.

Sand dunes and shingle banks are natural coastal defences, protecting low-lying land behind the beach from flooding by seawater. The strandline plants are the first line of defence and are quick to grow and reproduce. Their seeds are resistant to seawater and designed to fall deep into the substrate and lay dormant until conditions are suitable for germination, or to be carried away by the sea to colonise new beaches. These pioneer plants, therefore, if washed away in storms can quickly re-establish and start the whole process again.

Vegetated shingle beaches and sand dunes are threatened by seafront development and hard coastal defences such as sea walls and groynes, which prevent natural movement of these habitats. Hard structures at the back of the beach can cause coastal squeeze, where vegetation is unable to roll back landwards in the face of rising sea levels and is trapped in a narrow strip. Sand dunes are also under threat from mechanical cleaning of beaches, which removes the essential strandline debris and compacts the sand leaving a virtually barren environment.

The development of a healthy strandline is also important for a whole community of specialised invertebrates associated with the vegetation. The animals pollinate the plants, feed on them, lay their eggs on them and generally live there. Some are endemic to beach plants and are becoming extremely rare.

While there are numerous plants that live at the back of beaches, behind the strandline, the following pages describe those regularly found growing in amongst strandline debris. The best time to see these plants is generally between May and September when they are in flower or seed. Some die back completely in the winter. For further information about the vegetation of beaches we recommend buying a wildflower book.

Sea Sandwort *Honckenya peploides*

Height Stems to 25cm
A sprawling plant of sandy and shingle beaches, also growing on sand accumulating at the back of rocky beaches. The small, triangular, yellowish-green leaves are tightly and regularly arranged and the small, white flowers grow at the tip of each stem.

Prickly Saltwort *Salsola kali*

Height 20–60cm

Initially a sprawling plant but developing into a low-growing bush once established. The blue-green leaves are small and fleshy with a sharp spine at the tip. The pale yellow or pinkish flowers are small and insignificant, hidden at the base of the leaves. It is locally common on sandy beaches and is associated with the Sand Dart Moth, *Agrotis ripae*, whose larvae feed on it.

Sea Stock *Matthiola sinuata*

Height To 60cm

Can grow into a large, bushy, greyish-green plant, with narrow, toothed, velvety leaves and pink flowers. A mass of long seed pods develop throughout the flowering period giving the plant a distinctive appearance. It is found on sandy beaches at a few locations in the south and west of Britain.

Sea Beet *Beta vulgaris*

Height To 100cm

A low-growing plant with dark green, shiny leaves and reddish stems which grows all year round. A very common strandline plant found on any type of beach as well as other coastal habitats. The flowers, which lack petals, are green and arranged in spiky flower heads.

Sea Rocket *Cakile maritima*

Height 15–50cm

Can be sprawling or upright in form, with bluish-green, fleshy, toothed leaves and pale lilac or pink flowers. It grows on sand and shingle beaches, or where sand or cliff material accumulates on rocky beaches.

Sea Rocket seeds

Sea Rocket
sprawling form

Sea Kale *Crambe maritima*

Height 30–50cm

A large, bushy plant, with tough, cabbage-like, blue-green leaves and clusters of white flowers. The large seeds are designed to be distributed by the sea and are coated in a tough, buoyant material that is resistant to salt water. In winter the plant completely dies back above ground, leaving only a circular patch of organic material to mark the spot. However, the roots remain alive and in spring purple shoots start to emerge. It is predominantly a species of shingle beaches but can also be found where sand and stones accumulate.

Sea Kale overwintering stump

Rock Samphire *Crithmum maritimum*

Height To 45cm

A bushy plant with narrow, yellowish-green, fleshy leaves and clusters of yellowish flowers. It grows on stable shingle beaches but as a pioneer plant is best known from rocky shores, where it grows in areas where sand and strandline debris have accumulated.

Yellow Horned Poppy *Glaucium flavum*

Height to 90cm

A very distinctive and attractive plant of shingle beaches, with hairy, blue-green, lobed leaves forming a rosette from which the tall, branched stems emerge. The bright yellow, poppy flower is instantly recognisable, looking too delicate for such a wind-blown environment. Extremely long, thin seed pods develop from each flower head. These contain hundreds of tiny, black seeds which are fired out when the dried seed pod bursts, and fall into the gaps between the shingle. It is sometimes found growing on cliffs where there is loose material.

Oysterplant *Mertensia maritima*

Height Stems 30–60cm
A creeping plant, with blue-green, fleshy, oval leaves and tiny, bell-shaped flowers which change from pink to blue. The leaves reputedly taste of oysters. It grows on stony beaches. It is a rare, northern species, known from only a small number of locations in Scotland and Northern Ireland, having suffered decline.

Sea Mayweed *Tripleurospermum maritimum*

Height To 60cm
The flowers of this common seaside plant are daisy-like in appearance and colour. The leaves are feathery and slightly fleshy. It grows in clusters on sand and shingle beaches, including along the strandline.

Curled Dock *Rumex crispus*

Height 40–100cm
A widespread and common plant found in a variety of habitats where it prefers dry soils, and very common on strandlines. It is a tall plant with green, wavy-edged leaves and tall clusters of tiny, flowers which turn from green to rusty red in colour. In winter the stems turn woody and remain upright. The wavy-edged leaves are an adaptation to retain water.

Silverweed *Potentilla anserina*

This sprawling plant has yellow flowers which resemble buttercups. Its green or silvery-green leaves are fern-like in appearance, each with a number of toothed leaflets emerging in pairs either side of a main rib. It is not restricted to the coast but commonly grows in sandy soils and also on shingle beaches.

Orache *Atriplex* spp.

Frosted Orache
Atriplex laciniata

This group of plants is usually the first to colonise strandlines and they often appear as a green band just behind the high tide level. The species are difficult to tell apart and include Frosted Orache *Atriplex laciniata* (height 6–30cm), Babington's Orache *A. glabriuscula* (stems 10–100cm), Spear-leaved Orache *A. prostrata* (stems 10–100cm), and Grass-leaved Orache *A. littoralis* (stems 50–100cm).

They can be sprawling plants or upright, depending on the species, but all have green or silvery-green leaves and green, inconspicuous flowers. Leaves can be spear-shaped or narrow and both leaf types can be found on the same plant.

The orache family are ephemeral plants, typical of unstable environments where conditions may change or they may be washed away in a storm. They grow and produce seeds very quickly and may be very obvious on a beach one day and gone the next. On beaches where material is accumulating they are able to establish and this is when the succession of other vegetation takes over.

Spear-leaved
Orache, *Atriplex
prostrata*

Knotgrasses *Polygonum* spp.

Knotgrasses are plants of bare ground and a number of species, which are difficult to distinguish, can be found on strandlines. The small, oval leaves are arranged along the stems with small, white or pinkish flowers at their base. Papery sheaths form tubes enclosing the stem and leaf base.

Knotgrass *Polygonum aviculare*

This common species can be sprawling or low-growing, with oval, leathery leaves that are not rolled under.

Sea Knotgrass *Polygonum maritimum*

This rare plant grows along the ground and has oval leaves that are rolled under at the edges.

Ray's Knotgrass *Polygonum oxyspermum*

This sprawling plant has a limited distribution and has oval leaves that are only slightly rolled under at the edges.

Glossary

Amphipod a type of crustacean, generally small with a laterally flattened body.

Aperture opening, for example of a gastropod mollusc shell.

Bell (of a jellyfish) the umbrella-shaped dome of a jellyfish.

Bivalve a mollusc with a pair of hinged shells.

Bryozoan a type of colonial animal forming a structure in which the individual zooids live. The zooids produce tentacled lophophores for the capture of food. The structures of bryozoan colonies are extremely varied in size, shape and texture.

Byssus threads strong, fine threads made of protein, which are produced by some bivalve molluscs to attach themselves to hard substrates.

Carapace the part of a crab shell that covers the head and body.

Cephalopod a type of predatory marine mollusc, including octopus and squid, with a highly modified body. Cephalopods have tentacles for catching prey and an ink sac for defence. In most the shell is internal or absent.

Cetacean the group of marine mammals commonly known as whales, dolphins and porpoises. They breath air through a blow-hole on top of their head, have lost their hind limbs, the fore limbs are developed into flippers and they have a horizontal tail fluke.

Cnidaria a large and very varied group of animals including sea anemones, jellyfish, hydroids and corals, which all have stinging capsules or *nematocysts*. They have two major stages in their life-cycle; the medusa, free-swimming stage and the polyp, sessile (attached) stage.

Conservation Status (Red List) The International Union for the Conservation of Nature (IUCN) is the world authority on the conservation of plants and animals. It assesses the conservation status of individual species and produces lists stating which are in danger of extinction and which are less threatened. The Red List contains those species most threatened by extinction and in need of conservation.

Cryptic camouflaged and therefore difficult to spot in its natural environment.

Detritivore an animal which feeds on dead organic material.

Drift seeds plant seeds adapted for long-distance dispersal by water.

Elasmobranch a group of fish with a skeleton of cartilage and not bone, including the sharks, rays and skates.

Elytra the front pair of wings in beetles and some bugs, modified into hardened wing cases to protect the rear, flying pair of wings when not in use.

Endemic native or restricted to a particular place.

Gametes the male and female germ cells that combine in sexual reproduction.

Gastropod a type of mollusc with a single, often coiled, shell as in snails, or an internal or absent shell as in slugs.

Ghost fishing this term describes what happens when fishing gear continues to trap and kill animals after it has been lost in the sea.

Hilum the scar left on a seed or bean marking where it was attached to the inside of the pod.

Holdfast the part of a macro-alga or seaweed that anchors the plant to hard substrate.

Lophophore the tentacled feeding structure produced and used by byrozoans.

Mantle the body wall of a mollusc, which may be extended to form a siphon, for example in bivalves, or the foot in gastropods.

Medusa the jellyfish-like stage in the life-cycle of a cnidarian, which may be used for dispersal in sessile animals or as the main life stage, for example in jellyfish.

Nematocyst a type of stinging capsule used by cnidarians to poison or subdue their prey, or for defence.

Ocean gyre the rotation of oceanic water driven by currents. The currents at the outer edge of a gyre move more quickly than those nearer the centre. There are 11 major oceanic gyres on Earth and they exist in all the world's oceans.

Pelagic of the open sea or water column i.e. not living on the seabed or seashore.

Periostracum the flaky outer skin or coating on some bivalves.

Pleuston animals living at the interface between air and sea, the thin surface layer of the ocean. Their bodies project partly above the seas' surface.

Polyp the sea anemone-like sessile stage of cnidaria. This is the main life-stage of corals and hydroids.

Pharyngeal teeth structures in the throat of bony fish to help manipulate prey for swallowing. Some are designed for crushing hard structures such as bone and shell.

Photophores light-emitting organs often used by deep-water species living beyond the depths of light penetration in the ocean.

Radula the toothed, ribbon-like structure used by gastropods to rasp and break off particles of vegetable matter for ingestion.

Sessile an animal or colony of animals that is fixed or attached in one place.

Siphonophore a group of cnidarians that mainly have a free-swimming lifestyle. A siphonophore is actually a colony of individual zooids which have specialised functions ranging from reproduction and locomotion to capturing and processing prey.

Stipe the stalk-like part of a macro-alga or seaweed, as found in kelps.

Stranding a marine plant, animal or object washed up onto the seashore above the water line.

Telson the very last part or segment of a crustacean, sometimes forming a tail-fan as in shrimps or prawns.

Trophic level a feeding or consumer level in a food chain or food web.

Valve (of a bivalve) the single shell or half of hinged bivalve shell.

Ventral the lower side of an animal.

Zooid a single animal that is part of a colony, for example in a hydroid, bryozoan or coral.

Photographic credits

All photos are by Steve Trewhella except those stated below. The authors and publisher would like to thank those who have provided photographs.

Pages **23**, Shingle beach, Julie Hatcher; **40**, Sargasso weed, x2 Dr Paul Gainey; **41**, Sargasso Nudibranch, Norbert Wu/FLPA; **43**, Oyster Thief, Julie Hatcher; **62**, White Piddock, Amgueddfa Cymru – National Museum Wales; **107**, Spiny Starfish, Julie Dando; **137**, recording dead dolphin, Julie Hatcher; **141**, dead Grey Seal, Julie Hatcher; **142**, Leatherback Turtle carapace, Fergus Granville; **150**, Pearlside x2, Dr Lin Baldock; **154**, Oceanic Pufferfish, Richard Fabbri; **155**, Ocean Sunfish, Rob Holmes; **158**, driftwood, Julie Hatcher; **162**, nicker nut plant, Dr Paul Gainey; **170**, Fragile borer shell, Dr Paul Gainey; **188**, *Fiona pinnata*, Denis Riek; **214**, Steve holding fish conveyor, Julie Hatcher; **217**, complete Stone Crab trap, Dr Paul Gainey; **219**, Steve with buoys, Julie Hatcher; **222**, Steve holding high flyer, Julie Hatcher; **228**, Curt holding plastic ducks, Dave Ingraham; **230**, plastic soldier running, Julie Hatcher; **233**, blocked sewer, Thames Water; **235**, Steve in camo gear, Julie Hatcher; **238**, Steve holding Sand Hoppers, Julie Hatcher; **248**, pooter, Julie Hatcher; **289**, Sea Kale stump, Julie Hatcher; **291**, Oyster Plant, Sue Scott.

Further reading and websites

Bunker, F., Brodie, J., Maggs, C. & Bunker, A. 2012. *Seaweeds of Britain and Ireland.* Wild Nature Press.

Cleave, A. & Sterry, P. 2012. *Collins complete guide to British coastal wildlife.* Harper Collins Publishers Ltd.

Ebbesmeyer, C. & Scigliano, E. 2009. *Flotsametrics and the floating world.* Harper Collins Publishers Ltd.

Edwards, B. 2011. *The grasshoppers, bush-crickets and allies of Dorset.* Dorset Environmental Records Centre.

Harrap, S. 2013. *Harrap's Wild Flowers.* Bloomsbury Publishing Ltd.

Hayward, P. J. & Ryland, J. S. 1990. *The Marine Fauna of the British Isles and North-West Europe. Volume 1: Introduction to Protozoans and Arthropods.* Clarendon Press.

Hayward, P. J. & Ryland, J. S. 1995. *Handbook of the Marine Fauna of North-West Europe.* Oxford University Press.

Hayward, P., Nelson-Smith, T. & Shields, C. 1996. *Collins Pocket Guide – Seashore of Britain and Europe.* Harper Collins Publishers Ltd.

Holmes, A. M., Oliver P. G., Trewhella S., Hill R. & Quigley D. T. G. 2015. Trans-Atlantic rafting of inshore Mollusca on macro-litter: American molluscs on British and Irish shores. *Journal of Conchology* 42(1): 41–50.

Hopkin, S. 1991. *A key to the woodlice of Britain and Ireland.* Field Studies Council.

Hume, R. 2002. *RSPB Birds of Britain and Europe.* Dorling Kindersley Ltd.

Kay, P. & Dipper, F. 2009. *The Field Guide to the marine fishes of Wales and adjacent waters.* Marine Wildlife.

Kirby, R. R. 2010. *Ocean Drifters, a secret world beneath the waves.* Studio Cactus Ltd.

Kirkpatrick, P. A. & Pugh, P. R. 1984. *Siphonophores and velellids.* The Linnean Society of London.

Miller, P. J. & Loates, M. J. 1997. *Collins Pocket Guide to fish of Britain and Europe.* Harper Collins Publishers Ltd.

Naylor, P. 2011. *Great British Marine Animals (3rd Edition).* Sound Diving Publications.

Nelson, E. C. 2000. *Sea beans and Nickar nuts.* Botanical Society of the British Isles.

Norman, M. 2003. *Cephalopods – A World Guide.* Conch Books.

Picton, B. E. & Morrow, C. C. 1994. *A Field Guide to the Nudibranchs of the British Isles.* Immel Publishing Ltd.

Porter, J. 2012. *Seasearch guide to Bryozoans and Hydroids of Britain and Ireland.* Marine Conservation Society.

Winchester, S. 2012. *Skulls: An Exploration of Alan Dudley's Curious Collection.* Black Dog & Leventhal Publishers Inc.

Witherington, B. & D. 2007. *Florida's Living Beaches. A Guide for the Curious Beachcomber.* Pineapple Press Inc.

www.thewreckingseason.com A film by Nick and Jane Darke about their beachcombing exploits in Cornwall.

Index